THINKING, KNOWING, LIVING:

An Introduction to Philosophy

Edited by Richard A. Smith
Ball State University

University Press
of America™

Copyright © 1978 by

University Press of America™
division of
R.F. Publishing, Inc.
4710 Auth Place, S.E., Washington, D.C. 20023

Printed in the United States of America

ISBN: 0-8191-0492-2

CONTENTS

INTRODUCTION

WHAT IS PHILOSOPHY?

> *What we need is not the will to believe, but the wish to find out, which is exactly the opposite.*
> — Bertrand Russell

> A *very popular error: having the courage of one's convictions; rather it is a matter of having the courage for an* attack on *one's convictions.*
> -- Friedrich Nietzsche

The word 'philosophy' is derived from the Greek words *philos* (loving) and *sophia* (wisdom), and therefore can be defined as 'the love of wisdom'. This definition does little to describe the work and task of the professional philosopher, yet it rightly suggests that to a greater or lesser degree each of us in our own way can become a philosopher. We all have an interest in gaining wisdom.

1. *The subject matter of philosophy.* Unlike physics, chemistry, or math, there is in philosophy no specified 'content' to be learned, no set of facts or theories to be absorbed. In this respect philosophy is an art, its range being the entirety of all things human. In studying philosophy the practical import is not essentially in learning *what* but in learning *how*; namely, how to wonder, how to question, how to speculate, how to reason, how to critically evaluate--in short, how to inquire. Philosophy engages logical skill and creative imagination in the development of its inquiries.

No subject is too commonplace or remote to be devoid of philosophical interest. Areas of concern include science, theology, psychiatry, education, art, as well as law,medicine, and politics. Philosophy investigates basic issues regarding existence, God, and the nature of man; it seeks to know the difference between appearance and reality, the standards of good and evil, also the nature of truth, beauty, and justice.

The kinds of questions explored are those which aim to clarify the meanings of key terms, to uproot basic principles and underlying assumptions, to articulate conceptual relationships, and to examine methods of reasoning and standards of evaluation. The philosopher seeks to make explicit that which is merely implicit in various forms of experience and everyday types of thinking.

While it is true that everyone has the capability to philosophize, it is also true that like any art it can be done well or poorly. Experience and instruction will help improve one's philosophical skills. By reading classical philosophers and considering traditional problems, a person can develop and sharpen his reasoning abilities and powers of investigation. Ultimately, however, in dealing with philosophical issues each individual must come to grips with them for himself.

2. *Philosophy as an attitude.* In philosophy, as in any field where we seek knowledge and reliable guidance for conduct, objectivity is a requirement. In this context 'objectivity' connotes an attitude of open-mindedness and lack of prejudice. In forming our philosophical judgments we must carefully attend to the relevant evidence, we must not allow our emotions or biases to interfere with our investigations, and we must not discount ideas simply because they go against our intuitions. The mature philosophical attitude is expressed in the willingness to look at all sides of an issue.

To philosophize is not merely to read a lot of books or articles; it is to actually think, ponder, and reason about problems of human existence. Pursuit, searching out, questioning, inquiry—these are the keys to practicing philosophy. Here, too, the controlling factor is the philosopher's investigative and speculative attitude as he encounters difficult and perplexing problems.

The genuine philosophical attitude is one of reflection. Reflection is an ordered, regulated chain of thought, originating with some uncertainty, doubt, or curiosity, and impelling toward a conclusion or mental resolve. To reflect on some matter is to turn it over in one's mind, to *think it through,* with the implication that an entanglement is to be straightened out, an obscurity is to be clarified, a goal is to be reached. It involves purposefully reasoning out the ramifications of different views, then critically evaluating the alternatives. John Dewey sums it up by defining reflection as the "active, persistent, and careful consideration of any belief or supposed form of knowledge in the light of the grounds that support it and the further conclusions to which it tends."[1]

The method of reflection is precisely the method of inquiry. Its origin is some problem, i.e. some perplexity, curiosity, or doubt. What is my life and why am I here? What constitutes personal identity? Is man basically free, or is he the product of his heredity and socio-cultural environment? What is the relationship between my mind and body? What is the essence of justice? What distinguishes right from wrong? These are some traditional philosophical questions.

Given the specific problem, the next step is examination of the evidence and entertainment of possible solutions. Tentative theories of explanation are formulated and carefully developed. Since the immediate data itself is usually not sufficient to alleviate the problem, philosophical inquiry tends to move beyond the data by means of reasoning and inference. Here philosophy takes on the form of rational argumentation: philosophers are arguers. By an 'argument', however, is not meant a quarrel, but a strict, logically-developed inquiry, wherein definitions are clarified, assumptions tested, and implications pursued. Thus it is not unlike the sciences, where inquiry proceeds by the development of well-reasoned systematic theories to explain natural phenomena.

---

[1]John Dewey, *How We Think: A Restatement of the Relation of Reflective Thinking to the Educative Process* (Chicago: Henry Regnery Company, 1933), p. 9.

Finally, upon reaching a conclusion, the reflective attitude carries the full awareness that no solution is absolute. Again, just as scientific explanations cannot be thought of as final or ultimate, neither is it the case that philosophical inquiry yields the final truth of the matter. In no way can philosophy be conceived as providing a set of answers. The essence of philosophy is not the possession of truth, but the search for truth; its questions are more important than its answers, in fact every answer poses new questions. Philosophical reflection may not lead to certainty or total understanding, but the lack of reflection binds us to the prejudices of myth, ignorance, and illusion. The reflective attitude is the attitude of freedom; and to be free is to be able to question.

3. *Philosophy and common sense.* Philosophers consider 'commonsensical' those types of views widely held by ordinary people in their unreflective moments. Commonsense beliefs are those which seem 'intuitively' obvious. It is a matter of common sense that if you receive a letter in the mail then someone must have sent it. We believe that other people have thoughts, feelings, and emotions similar to our own, and that these experiences can be accurately conveyed by language. Still more basically, we firmly believe that we have a body, that the sun came up today, and that this book will continue to exist even when nobody is reading it or perceiving it.

In spite of the fact that they sometimes turn out to be mistaken or only partly true, these and other commonsense convictions form a nucleus around which the totality of man's practical life is built. Without this nucleus we simply could not get on with our everyday affairs. What, then, is the relationship between common sense and philosophy?

In the first place there seems to be a difference in attitude. Whereas the dominant attitude of common sense is one of *acceptance*, that of philosophy is one of questioning. Common sense exhibits a willingness to take things at face value; the very nature of philosophy is to penetrate beneath the surface. We commonly believe in the existence of material objects such as trees and buildings—what could be more obvious! Bishop Berkeley, however, who we will study later, seriously challenged this kind of belief, and he did so by questioning the very foundations of human experience. Whether Berkeley was right

4

or wrong is not the point; but here is an extreme example where a given philosophy expresses itself as a critique of common sense.

Now the main purpose of philosophy is not to undermine common sense. In fact, for some philosophers the very goal is to rationally justify basic commonsense beliefs, by methods of clarifying the language used to express the beliefs. But why is there a need to defend common sense? Why is it the target of so much criticism? The reason is that, its utility notwithstanding, common sense is prone to confusion, ambiguity, inconsistency, and error.

Common sense would have it that killing is morally wrong, but it is often hard-pressed to sufficiently explain why. We say that a penny looks circular and a box appears to have six sides, even though a penny truly appears circular only when viewed from directly above the center at a perpendicular angle, and though we never actually 'see' more than three sides of the box at the same time. We believe we are *free* to act as we choose, yet we also believe that a person's character is *determined* by genetic and environmental factors: seemingly contradictory positions. We believe that physical objects exist independently of being perceived, yet the only objects we can ever prove to exist are those we perceive. We believe we accurately know about happenings which were experienced in the past, yet how often does it happen that our memory is mistaken! These and other examples render many everyday commonsense ideas philosophically problematic.

Again it must be emphasized that philosophy is not out to denigrate common sense. The aim--as always--is toward wisdom. Just as the scientist starts at the surface and systematically penetrates beneath in order to obtain detailed knowledge of objects, organisms, relationships, and so forth, so it is with the philosopher, who begins at the outer edge and works inward, probing, questioning, inquiring. And the outer edge is none other than common sense. By paying heed to common sense, also by identifying pitfalls and weaknesses, the reflective individual is able to become more discerning, more critical, indeed, more intelligent.

What, then, is philosophy? . . .

　　　Philosophy is the eternal search for truth, a search which inevitably fails and yet is never defeated; which continually eludes us, but which always guides us. This free, intellectual life of the mind is the noblest inheritance of the Western world; it is also the hope of our future.
　　　　　　　　　　　　　　　　　-- W. T. Jones

CHAPTER ONE

PERCEIVING AND KNOWING

SOME PROBLEMS OF PHILOSOPHY

> The *true lover of knowledge is always striving after* being. . . . *He will not rest at those multitudinous phenomena whose existence is appearance only.*
> —Plato

INTRODUCTION

Epistemology is a branch of philosophy defined as the study of human knowledge. Through a careful examination of the sources, nature, and limits of our knowledge, we can begin to develop a more informed understanding of what we know and don't know.

Our knowledge is basically of two sorts: *empirical* and *rational*. Empirical knowledge includes all that is known by way of sense experience or observation. As exploratory organs, our senses provide a major link or means for becoming acquainted with the world in which we live. By sense experience we learn that sugar is sweet and lemons are not, that dogs bark and cats meow, that the sky is blue, water is wet, snow is white, and that skunks smell different than French perfume. Furthermore it is evident that all science is founded upon empirical observation and experimentation.

Rational knowledge refers to what is known through the use of reason, and usually involves deriving new information from prior data. The two general forms of reasoning are *deduction* and *induction*. Deduction is the logical process of drawing out (or deducing) the implications of one or more premises or statements of fact. If a given deductive argument is *valid*, the truth of the premises necessarily implies the truth

of the conclusion. For example, given the truth of the two
premises, "All men are mortal," and "Socrates is a man," it
therefore follows necessarily that "Socrates is mortal." Deduction in its exact form occurs primarily in mathematics,
geometry, and symbolic logic.

Induction, on the other hand, is a logical procedure for
inferring a general conclusion from a set of particular facts.
After having observed twenty swans, for instance, all of which
were white, I might inductively infer that all swans are white.
As applied in science, induction is a way of projecting ex-
planatory laws or principles—e.g. the law of gravity, or
Newton's laws of motion—on the basis of only a finite number
of actual observations. Notice, however, that inductive inferences are always tentative, never absolute, always subject
to change in the light of additional data. The next swan I
see might be black, thus shattering my initial conclusion. So
whereas deduction leads to necessity or certainty, induction
never provides more than *probable* knowledge. Indeed, the
greater number of cases examined, the greater the probability
of the conclusion—but it's strictly a probability nevertheless.

The senses and reason thus constitute the primary sources
of knowledge. The next step is to determine the nature of such
knowledge. That is, what sort of knowledge is actually achieved?
Is it knowledge of a world of *things*, existing independently of
our perceiving or conceiving them, a real, objective world outside the mind? The instinctive and commonsense view, called
naive realism, takes it for granted that this is the case.
There are some philosophers, however, Berkeley for one, who
argue that things have no existence except *for perceivers*, that
mind (or consciousness) is the only reality. Such philosophers
are called *idealists*. Before making any rash judgments, it
would do well to inquire why anyone should abandon realism in
its simplest form. We shall soon see that the world is much
more complicated than the unreflective man supposes.

In daily life, the most natural assumption is that things,
i.e. tables, chairs, trees, mushrooms, and all the rest, exist
prior to and independently of anyone's perceiving them; and
that, when we do perceive them, we perceive them directly, as
they are *in themselves*, that is, exactly as they would be if
nobody were perceiving them. For example, this book is really,

10

physically here, whether anyone is looking at it or not; it is really oblong, of a certain definite size, and having a certain definite color; it is really hard and smooth-surfaced. Purportedly all of this is proven because sense experience empirically shows that it is so. Furthermore, it is most natural to assume that the same object—this book—can be directly known and perceived by more than one person. The realistic assumption throughout is that the objective world exists as a *given,* and that its nature is truly revealed through sensible experience.

However, there are definite problems that arise in sense perception. Take the sense of sight. I look at a certain tabletop, it appears to be brown. But where or what is color? Although I believe the table is 'really' the same color all over, the parts that reflect the light look brighter than the other parts. And if I move, the parts that reflect the light will be different, the apparent distribution of colors on the tabletop will change. Likewise if several people are perceiving the table at the same time, it is obvious that no two of them will experience exactly the same distribution of colors, because two people cannot occupy the same space at the same time, and any change in point of view makes some change in the way the light is reflected.[1]

If I put on blue-colored glasses, the world looks blue. If I put on red glasses, the world looks red. What appears red to a person with normal vision, appears grayish to someone who is color-blind. To a person suffering from jaundice everything seems yellowish. Yet in none of these cases has anything been done to the 'outer' world.

There is a coin on my desk. People say it is circular, but from most points of view it looks elliptical. We believe the table is really rectangular, but from most points of view it will appear as a parallelogram. If two lines are parallel, they will appear to converge at some point in the distance. These examples and others lead to an important yet often

---

[1]This illustration is from Bertrand Russell, *The Problems of Philosophy* (New York: Oxford University Press, 1959), chapter 1.

troublesome philosophical distinction—that between *appearance* and *reality*, between what things seem to be and what they are. The practical man as well as the philosopher is interested in knowing things as they really are, though the philosopher's interest is usually stronger and he is more troubled by the difficulties involved.

To return to the color of the table. It is evident from our analysis that there is no color which appears to be *the* color of the table *in and of itself*, since it appears to be different colors from different points of view, under different conditions, to different people; while in the dark there is no color at all. The color we perceive is not something inherent in the physical table itself. The physiological fact is that light strikes the surface of the table which, due to the molecular structure of the material, reflects back certain electromagnetic waves that stimulate the retinas of our eyes which in turn send impulses to the visual centers of the cortex, *where they are interpreted as colors*. In short, the color we see depends upon the nature of our eyes.

From the above, two conclusions must be drawn which are of utmost significance for understanding the nature of perception.

(1) Color is an experience in our minds. It is the product of a long and complicated process of conversion and interpretation.

(2) There is no color whatsoever in physical objects themselves. The table only *appears* to be brown. *Really,* the table is not brown, the sky is not blue, snow is not white, and there is no color in the rainbow.

Furthermore, these conclusions hold true for all our senses, and for all possible senses we might imagine. With the sense of touch, whether the stimulus be pressure or pain, heat or cold, *what* is perceived is the product of various operations in the cerebral cortex. There is no 'sweetness' in the chocolate candy, no 'sourness' in the lemon. And the tree that falls in a forest when nobody is around makes nary a sound: it might create a lot of waves in the air, but lest these waves be converted and interpreted—there can be no

12

sound. In a word, were there no sentient beings in existence, there would be no colors, no sounds, no odors.

This preliminary analysis of perception has inevitable and devastating consequences for simple realism. Where the commonsense realist intuitively believes that sense perception conveys an accurate description of the way things *really* are, it is now clear that the immediate objects of sensation—colors, sounds, odors, etc.—are not an actual part of the antecedently existing physical things themselves, but rather in some way are organ-produced. Even supposing there is an independently existing physical world 'out there'—which has yet to be proven—we cannot *directly* reach it by the senses, or by any empirical means. Naive realism just is not an adequate theory of knowledge.

Before proceeding further, it will be helpful to specify the meaning of a few simple terms we shall have occasion to use. The name 'sense-data' will be used to refer to those things immediately known through sense experience: such things as colors, tastes, sounds, odors, and so on. The word 'sensation' will refer to the actual experience of being directly aware of sense-data. A sensation is a state of consciousness, where the object of such consciousness is one or more sense-data. Thus, whenever we see a color, we *have* a sensation of the color, but the color itself is a sense-*datum*, not a sensation. And if we use the term 'physical object' to refer to real things in the world, it follows that sense-data are to be construed as non-physical or mental objects, in that they depend upon some mind for their very existence.

The failure of commonsense realism raises anew the question how we are to acquire knowledge of the external world, assuming, of course, that such a world really exists. From our previous reasoning, it is plain that sense experience never gives us direct acquaintance with the real properties of physical objects. Our senses do not convey truths about reality—only about appearance. Reality is never anything we experience; at best, it is something *inferred* from what we experience. Following along these lines, although it is true that sensation does not reveal *directly* any definite property of a physical object, we might infer that sense-data are possibly *signs* of certain real properties which perhaps *cause* particular sensations, without ever

13

being actually apparent in these sensations. In other words, the suggestion is offerred that knowledge of reality is possible only by indirect means.

Two very difficult questions at once arise: (1) Are there such things as independently existing physical objects? (2) If so, what is the relationship between physical objects and sense-data? More generally, the issue concerns the relationship between reality and appearance. What is needed is a type of theory that incorporates a rational means for linking empirical data with material objects, thus supplying indirect—though rationally justifiable—knowledge of the external world. But what sort of theory could this be? If we never experience anything but appearance, and if reality is not the same as appearance, then how can we be sure there is any reality at all? Even if there is, how can we ever truly come to know what it is like?

These are bewildering questions, especially when considering that prior to our critical reflection the matter seemed so simple and commonsensical. Philosophy may not satisfactorily answer as many questions as we would like; still, its primary value is in raising questions which foster new interest in the world we so often take for granted, questions which reveal the strangeness and wonder in even the most ordinary daily experiences.

To help broaden our perspective, the next step will be to consider some alternative epistemological theories concerning the relationship between appearance and reality, and the plausibility of attaining knowledge of the physical world by means of sense-data.

SCEPTICISM

Roughly defined, scepticism is the view that knowledge of reality is impossible, that the 'physical world' is beyond the reach of human cognition; hence, that all claims to know reality are ultimately without justification. Negative in its formulation and radical in its conclusion, scepticism is alien to our most intuitive inclinations. This in itself, however, should not count as an objection, for we already know from the preceding that our commonsense intuitions are subject to error. Thus we need to seriously examine the reasons given in defense of scepticism, and only then will it be possible to render a well-considered judgment regarding the theory, pro or con.

We already have ruled out the possibility of directly knowing reality by empirical means; but scepticism goes even further by discounting any possibility for indirect knowledge of reality as well. The aim of the sceptic is to demonstrate the existence of an unbridgeable gap between the conclusion which we seek—knowledge of the external world—and the premises with which we begin, i.e. propositions relating exclusively to our sense experience. First of all, he argues, since the conclusion of a valid deduction can contain no reference to entities which do not already figure in its premises, it follows that there can be no deductive passage from the experience of sense-data to knowledge of physical objects.

If the gap cannot be bridged by a deductive process, the sceptic continues, it must, therefore, involve some kind of inductive inference, one in which the conclusion goes beyond the premises, as in the case of deriving an empirical generalization from the observance of particular instances. Yet, to the extent that inductive reasoning is legitimate at all, it can carry us forward only on the same level. That is, on the basis of past experiences induction may indeed lead us to generalizations regarding possible future experiences, but in no way can it logically lead to the existence of any object that transcends experience. By observing cats we cannot be led to inductive generalizations about dogs. Similarly, inductive reasoning cannot justify a passage from the occurrence of sense-data to the existence of objects which are *not* sense-data., i.e. physical objects.

Therefore, he concludes, since knowledge of the external world cannot be achieved by direct empirical means, nor either by deductive or inductive reasoning, it follows that such knowledge is simply impossible. All of which means, if he is right, that our very belief in the existence of a physical world has neither empirical nor rational warrant.

To a casual reader scepticism probably appears as an insane and utterly ridiculous view: who in his right mind—except some crazy philosopher-type—would really ever go to such an extreme as to cast open doubt upon the existence of

15

the external world? But scepticism is more than a mere aca-
demic exercise, and it deserves to be taken seriously. In our
own everyday lives, who of us has not experienced moments of
doubt, moments when we seem unable to come up with a solid,
fixed point that can give us support in our beliefs and ideals?
Such feelings are unique to each individual, thus difficult
to convey in a general sense; but they exist nevertheless. The
difference between the sceptic and you or I is that in these
brief though 'revealing' moments he sees a reflection of the
permanent cognitive condition of human existence. Where you
and I soon return to the ordinary way of seeing things, the
sceptic regards this as a return to delusion.

       Is it possible to ever know reality; or must we resign
ourselves to groping in the dark, with no prospect of achieving
true understanding of the world in which we live? The importance of scepticism, at least if nothing else, is in drawing
attention to this fundamental philosophical issue. What our
final position will be will depend on how adequately we are
able to overcome the sceptic's argument; and that, in turn,
will depend on how satisfactorily we are able to show that
knowledge of reality is indeed possible. The task is now
clearly laid out before us.

REPRESENTATIVE REALISM:
A CAUSAL THEORY OF PERCEPTION

       One reply to scepticism is of the sort given by John Locke,
among others. Since later on in this chapter there is a se-
lected reading from Locke, the following comments will be of
a general nature.

       First, it can be agreed that there is a distinction be-
tween the way things appear and the way they really are, and
also that sense-data must be distinguished from physical objects,
only the latter of which have an existence independent of the
mind. Although many objects look colored and carry an odor,
we can readily admit that they are not really colored or oder-
iferous at all. But as against the sceptic, it is claimed, we
can reasonably and justifiably say about such objects that *they
have the capacity* of *causing* in human beings the look of being
colored and the appearance of a certain odor. And this becomes
the basis for our knowledge about reality.

16

According to this *causal theory of perception,* while it is perfectly proper to say that an object is red, what this *means* is that the object has a certain causal property—i.e. the property of causing a normal observer viewing from an ordinary point of view under usual conditions of light to see a red appearance. Within the framework of this widely-held theory, the relationship between appearance and reality is resolved in terms of causation, and, likewise, the sceptic's chasm between sense-data and physical objects is overcome by a causal bridge.

In this connection it is generally argued that physical objects have certain 'real' properties which are totally independent of any act of perception, qualities like size, weight, molecular structure. In Locke's terminology these are called *primary properties;* these are properties which modern physics ascribes to material objects. Even if an object such as a table is not being perceived, it still has a certain weight and molecular structure.

Other properties, which objects appear to have but do not have (except in the sense of corresponding causal powers), are called *secondary.* An object may not 'really' have the property of redness, although in virtue of its material texture (and other primary qualities) it does have the potency or power to produce in us the sense-datum red, as long as other requisite perceptual conditions are satisfied.

Still, if our only experiential contact with the physical world is by way of secondary properties which, strictly speaking, are not actually properties of physical objects at all, it has yet to be shown how such 'contact' leads to genuine knowledge of the external world. Simply pointing out that an object has a certain capacity or potency does not seem sufficiently descriptive.

Many philosophers, including Locke, maintain that while sense-data are not identical with, or even any part of, material objects, there exists between the two a fundamental relationship of *representation.* This is called the *representational theory of perception,* and usually is espoused in conjunction with the causal theory. The basic idea is analogous to the process of photography: experiential sense-data, like

17

developed photographs, while not identical with the 'real' things, are close 'copies'. And just as we can learn about and come to know things by way of photographs, so too, goes the argument, can we come to know reality by way of sense-data.

Such arguments, however, are far from satisfactory. First off, assuming that a given sense-datum stems from a certain 'external' cause—and that's a big assumption!—what justifiable reason do we have to claim that such cause, (1) is an actual property of a physical object, or (2) has an existence independent of sensation? Secondly, the apparent distinction between primary and secondary properties is riddled with problems, and as we will see in a later reading, Berkeley persuasively explains that primary qualities are no less mind-dependent that are secondary qualities—which is a stiff jolt to any realist theory of knowledge. Thirdly, even if we admit that sense-data somehow are 'copies' of reality, how do we truly know that the real thing is anything at all like the copy? Pictures frequently distort an actual setting. Sometimes cameras malfunction, producing defective photos. How do we know that our senses are perfect receivers? In the case of two people having dissimilar sense experiences of supposedly the same object, whose sense-data are more truly representative? In fact, how can anyone ever know that two things (sense-datum and physical object) resemble one another, if we are theoretically incapable of experiencing one of the two (i.e. the physical object)? Such unanswered questions have led philosophers to investigate alternatives to representative realism.

SUBJECTIVE IDEALISM

Recall the charge of the sceptic, that an unbridgeable gap exists between sense-data and reality. A most unique reply is to simply 'reduce' reality to the status of sense-data, hence disrupting any need for a bridge. This is the course taken by those philosophers called subjective idealists, the most notable of whom is Bishop George Berkeley.

Idealism is a world view which holds that reality consists primarily of minds and ideas (or sense-data). While the term 'idealism' is used differently by different philosophers, and while as a full-blown theory it historically has taken on a

variety of forms, for present purposes we shall define idealism
as the doctrine that whatever exists, or at any rate whatever
can be known to exist, must be in some sense mental, or mind-
dependent.

Objects of experience, therefore, are not considered physical in nature, but mental, subjective. Indeed, things such
as trees and buildings exist, but they are said to exist only
in a mind that perceives them. In other words, idealism funda-
mentally denies that reality exists independently of minds.
Notice here that the words 'existence' and 'reality' are used
in a special sense, quite differently from the way they are
used ordinarily.

To people not accustomed to philosophical speculation,
idealism—just as scepticism—probably seems absurd. But
whether true or false, idealism is not to be dismissed without
carefully examining the arguments presented in its defense.
What these arguments are we will come to in a later selection
wherein Berkeley presents his theory in his own words. Still,
a few critical problems seem worth discussing beforehand.

If the idealist analysis is correct, the logical result
would seem to be *solipsism*—the view that nothing is known to
exist except my own experience, that everything else is just
an extension of my subjective consciousness. According to
solipsism, other people and objects exist only in my mind: when
I stop perceiving them or thinking about them, they cease to
exist!

Solipsism cannot strictly be proven to be false, and there
is no logical impossibility in the supposition that the whole
of life is a dream, in which we ourselves create all the objects
that come before us. Practically speaking, however, no person
could ever live his life as a solipsist. As we learned earlier
regarding common sense, belief in the external world and the
existence of other people is a requisite for getting on in life.
Thus, although solipsism is logically possible, there doesn't
seem to be any legitimate grounds for supposing it is true.
Whereas, on the other hand, if a given theory ultimately leads
to solipsism, that would count as at least one objection to
the theory. Such may be the case with Berkeley's idealism.

19

To avoid such an extreme as solipsism, however, Berkeley relies on an outside source for his ideas: God. Objects continue to exist even when I am not perceiving them, says Berkeley, because God is perceiving them, they exist in God's mind. Furthermore, the very order and consistency of the natural world is due to God's governing perception. This explains why many people are able to perceive the 'same' objects, and why we cannot determine merely by willing it what we shall see when we open our eyes. With this line of reasoning, unfortunately, other problems arise, the chief one being: how can I ever know that God exists (outside of my mind)?

Other important questions to keep in mind when reading Berkeley include: What is a mind? How can I know that my mind or any mind exists? What is the difference between imagination and perception? Is there any difference between 'true' perception and erroneous perception (illusion, hallucination, etc.)? If so, how can we tell?

PHENOMENALISM, SCIENCE, AND KNOWLEDGE

A somewhat different method of escaping scepticism is to show that knowledge of reality can be inductively derived from particular sense experiences, to the extent that the cognitive conclusions are formulated as scientific hypotheses subject to empirical verification. This type of theory is defended by A. J. Ayer in his book, *The Foundations of Empirical Knowledge.*

Let us begin with a question: can there be conceived any empirical situation which is sufficient to establish the existence of a physical object? If the answer is no, then scepticism is inescapable. While if the answer is yes, the task becomes one of describing what that situation would be like. Let this be our goal.

Lest we adopt some form of idealism, we must suppose that the term 'physical object' is not synonymous with any term or set of terms that stand for sense-data. We already know that the only objects ever immediately perceived are sense-data. We must therefore surmise that if it is possible to empirically establish the existence of physical objects, it must be in terms of sense-data. Yet, from previous discussion we also know that strictly on the basis of that which is observed (i.e. sense-data)

20

it is impossible to validly infer the existence of anything conceived as being, in principle, unobservable (i.e. physical objects). Is there any way to resolve this apparent dilemma?

Those philosophers called *phenomenalists* take the position that although physical objects are not identical with or definable as a collection of actual and possible sense-data, "any proposition that refers to a material thing must somehow be expressible in terms of sense-data,if it is to be empirically significant."[1] It is primarily a linguistic claim, namely, that sentences referring to physical objects are, in theory, translatable into sentences referring exclusively to sense-data. Whereas for a Berkelian idealist the reality of an object is necessarily confirmed by its being perceived, according to phenomenalism, as will be explained, having a certain sensation does not guarantee the existence of a physical object, but *it does count as evidence.*

Consider an analogy. A pathologist or bacteriologist talks of tuberculosis. It is the name of a specific disease that exists and from which people really die. But has anyone actually 'seen' or 'touched' or 'tasted' tuberculosis? Of course not, it is not the kind of thing that can be perceived by the senses. So why do medical doctors believe in its existence? Because there is evidence available, that is, there are symptoms which are standard for determining cases of TB. Now just because a patient has one of the symptoms, that does not prove he has TB—but it counts as evidence. If the patient has two or three of the symptoms, that is greater evidence; and if he has all the classic symptoms, the probabilities are extremely high for having the disease, though even here it is not an absolute certainty. Philosophically speaking, TB is not identical with any or all of the external symptoms, but the presence of the latter is relevant to establishing the existence of the former. In a sense, the word 'tuberculosis' can be conceived as a name for a *logical construction* from a set of external symptoms.

---

[1]A. J. Ayer, *The Foundations of Empirical Knowledge* (New York: St. Martin's Press, Inc., 1955), p. 231.

Why not approach the existence of physical objects in a similar manner, namely, as logical constructions out of sense-data? We believe in the existence of material objects, though in principle they are unobservable. Yet, why not count as evidence certain types of empirical data? Propositions about physical objects would therefore be treated as scientific hypotheses, which may be confirmed or discredited by actual sense experience. For example, a statement such as "There is a table in the room" is to be regarded as an hypothesis subject to empirical verification by way of sense experience. Possible verifying experiences include having a certain visual table-appearance, getting an affirmative response from other people in the room who also 'see' the table, having corroborating tactile sensations if I proceed to touch the table, or sit on it, or kick it, etc. On the other hand, if I go to touch the table which I see, but find 'nothing there'—this would suggest the probability of illusion or hallucination.

According to the phenomenalist, when people speak of 'perceiving a physical object' what is involved is a (conscious or unconscious) process of inference from the occurrence of one sense-datum to the possible occurrence of another. To say that I am perceiving a tree means: 1) I am experiencing certain sense-data; 2) I am assuming the possibility of obtaining further 'confirming' sense-data. This is not to claim that the physical object simply is a set of sense-data; rather, that the actualization of a series of inferred experiential possibilities counts as empirical evidence in favor of the reality-hypothesis implicit in the initial perception. Hence, through verifying experiences we are able to achieve knowledge of reality.

What does it mean to say that an empirical hypothesis has been verified? We can look to science for the answer. In so far as the function of an hypothesis is to enable us in predicting and anticipating types of experience, if an observation or experience conforms to our expectations, the truth of the given hypothesis is therein verified. Like the scientist, we must realize that verification can never be considered absolute or final, since it is always possible that some future experience will discredit the original hypothesis.

22

Suppose we accept the phenomenalistic-scientific view that statements about physical objects are to be understood as empirical hypotheses translatable in terms of possible sense experiences. It follows that in any given instance we can be said to have knowledge of the material world precisely in the degree to which the hypothesis is experientially verified. It also follows that statements about physical objects are never conclusively verified, and thus can never be known with certainty. The more tests that are performed, and the more times our expectations are fulfilled, the greater is the probability that our belief is true. But the fact remains, since the number of possible tests is infinite, that however many favorable tests are made, the stage will never be reached at which it ceases to be conceivable that some further test will reverse the verdict of the previous evidence. And the same holds with respect to falsifying an hypothesis. This characteristic of verification and falsification is fully recognized and accepted by scientists, so as philosophers why not let us do likewise?

An overall evaluation of phenomenalism is not easy. On the positive side, it offers an alternative to scepticism. Also it does not involve the intrinsic difficulties of the causal theory; the phenomenalist is not concerned with the cause of our sense-data, but with hypotheses regarding the occurrence of further sense-data. And it has advantages over the representational theory, primarily since there is no need to determine whether sense-data are accurate copies of reality. Furthermore, in contrast with most forms of idealism, phenomenalism does not ultimately lead to solipsism.

At the same time, phenomenalism has its own difficulties. Most obviously, it operates on the premise that knowledge about reality is never certain but at best a probability. This is offensive to those who maintain that for knowledge *to be knowledge* it must be certain. Also the sceptic might jump in and argue that if we cannot obtain certainty, then we cannot have knowledge of reality.

Another objection stems from the phenomenalistic claim that the physical world is a 'logical construction' out of sense-data. Not only does such a claim go counter to common sense, but it suggests that the material world is something we *create*—as if we had some choice in the matter. Maybe phenomenalism is just a sophisticated form of idealism.

Phenomenalism, just as any other theory, is not unprob-
lematical. One mark of its adequacy is how well it can defend
itself in light of the above types of criticism.

SUMMARY

The preceding has been an introduction to the subject of
epistemology and some of the issues it deals with. The two
main sources of knowledge have been outlined, and the question
has been raised regarding the possibility of acquiring knowledge of reality. In this context a number of traditional
theories have been discussed and briefly evaluated. These
constitute only a small number of the many epistemological
theories brought forth throughout the history of philosophy,
and the ones we have considered are not necessarily the most
widely accepted or most defensible. They do, however, provide
a diverse glimpse of the philosophical mind at work.

JOHN LOCKE

A CAUSAL THEORY OF PERCEPTION

OF IDEAS IN GENERAL

1. *Idea is the object of thinking* .—Every man being conscious to himself that he thinks, and that which his mind is
applied about whilst thinking being the ideas that are there,
it is past doubt that men have in their minds several ideas,
such as are those expressed by the words, 'whiteness, hardness,
sweetness, thinking, motion, man, elephant, army, drunkenness',
and others. It is in the first place then to be inquired, How
he comes by them?

2. *All ideas come from sensation or reflection.*—Let us
then suppose the mind to be, as we say, white paper, void of
all characters, without any ideas; how comes it to be furnished?
Whence comes it by that vast store, which the busy and boundless fancy of man has painted on it with an almost endless
variety? Whence has it all the materials of reason and knowledge? To this I answer, in one word, from EXPERIENCE; in that
all our knowledge is founded, and from that it ultimately derives itself. Our observation, employed either about external
sensible objects, or about the internal operations of our minds,
perceived and reflected on by ourselves, is that which supplies
our understandings with all the materials of thinking. These
two are the fountains of knowledge, from whence all the ideas
we have or can naturally have, do spring.

3. *The objects of sensation one source of ideas.*--
First, our senses, conversant about particular sensible objects,
do convey into the mind several distinct perceptions of things,

---

From John Locke, *An Essay Concerning Human Understanding*,
first published in 1690.

25

according to those various ways wherein those objects do affect them; and thus we come by those *ideas* we have of yellow, white, heat, cold, soft, hard, bitter, sweet, and all those which we call sensible qualities; which when I say the senses convey into the mind, I mean, they from external objects convey into the mind what produces there those perceptions. This great source of most of the ideas we have, depending wholly upon our senses, and derived by them to the understanding, I call, SENSATION.

4. *The operations of our minds the other source of them.*-- Secondly, the other fountain, from which experience furnisheth the understanding with ideas, is the perception of the operations of our mind within us, as it is employed about the ideas it has got; which operations, when the soul comes to reflect on and consider, do furnish the understanding with another set of ideas which could not be had from things without: and such are thinking, doubting, believing, reasoning, knowing, willing, and all the different actings of our own minds; which we being conscious of, and observing in ourselves, do from these receive into our understanding as distinct ideas, as we do from bodies affecting our senses. This source of ideas every man has wholly in himself: and though it be not sense, as having nothing to do with external objects, yet it is very like it, and might properly enough be called internal sense. But as I call the other Sensation, so I call this REFLECTION, the ideas it affords being such only as the mind gets by reflecting on its own operations within itself.

SOME FURTHER CONSIDERATIONS CONCERNING OUR SIMPLE IDEAS

1. *Positive ideas from privative causes.*--Concerning the simple ideas of sensation it is to be considered, that whatsoever is so constituted in nature as to be able by affecting our senses to cause any perception in the mind, doth thereby produce in the understanding a simple idea; which, whatever be the external cause of it, when it comes to be taken notice of by our discerning faculty, it is by the mind looked on and considered there to be a real positive idea in the understanding, as much as any other whatsoever; though perhaps the cause of it be but a privation in the subject.

2. Thus the ideas of heat and cold, light and darkness, white and black, motion and rest, are equally clear and positive ideas in the mind. . . . These the understanding, in its view of them, considers all as distinct positive ideas without taking notice of the causes that produce them: which is an inquiry not belonging to the idea as it is in the understanding, but to the nature of the things existing without us. These are two very different things, and carefully to be distinguished; it being one thing to perceive and know the idea of white or black, and quite another to examine what kind of particles they must be, and how ranged in the superficies, to make any object appear white or black.

7. *Ideas in the mind, qualities in bodies.*—To discover the nature of our ideas the better, and to discourse of them intelligibly, it will be convenient to distinguish them, as they are ideas or perceptions in our minds, and as they are modifications of matter in the bodies that cause such perceptions in us; that so we may not think (as perhaps usually is done) that they are exactly the images and resemblances of something inherent in the subject; most of those of sensation being in the mind no more the likeness of something existing without us than the names that stand for them are the likeness of our ideas, which yet upon hearing they are apt to excite in us.

8. Whatsoever the mind perceives in itself, or is the immediate object of perception, thought, or understanding, that I call *idea*; and the power to produce any idea in our mind, I call *quality* of the subject wherein that power is. Thus a snowball having the power to produce in us the ideas of white, cold, and round, the powers to produce those ideas in us as they are in the snowball, I call qualities; and as they are sensations or perceptions in our understandings, I call them ideas; which ideas, if I speak of them sometimes as in the things themselves, I would be understood to mean those qualities in the objects which produce them in us.

9. *Primary qualities of bodies.*—Qualities thus considered in bodies are, First, such as are utterly inseparable from the body, in what estate soever it be; such as, in all the alterations and changes it suffers, all the force can be used upon it, it constantly keeps; and such as sense constantly finds in

27

every particle of matter which has bulk enough to be perceived, and the mind finds inseparable from every particle of matter, though less than to make itself singly be perceived by our senses: v.g., take a grain of wheat, divide it into two parts, each part has still solidity, extension, figure, and mobility; divide it again, and it retains still the same qualities: and so divide it on, till the parts become insensible; they must retain still each of them all those qualities. . . . These I call *original* or *primary qualities* of body, which I think we may observe to produce simple ideas in us, viz. solidity, extension, figure, motion or rest, and number.

10. *Secondary qualities of bodies.*—Secondly, such qualities, which in truth are nothing in the objects themselves, but powers **to** produce various sensations in us by their primary qualities, i.e., by the bulk, figure, texture, and motion of their insensible parts, as colors, sounds, tastes, &c., these I call *secondary qualities.* To these might be added a third sort, which are allowed to be barely powers, though they are as much real qualities in the subject as those which I, to comply with the common way of speaking, call qualities, but, for distinction, secondary qualities. For the power in fire to produce a new color or consistence in wax or clay by its primary qualities, is as much a quality in fire as the power it has to produce in *me* a new idea or sensation of warmth or burning, which I felt not before, by the same primary qualities, viz., the bulk, texture, and motion of its insensible parts.

11. *How primary qualities produce their ideas.*—The next thing to be considered is, how bodies produce ideas in us; and that is manifestly by impulse, the only way which we can conceive bodies operate in.

12. If, then, external objects be not united to our minds when they produce ideas in it, and yet we perceive these original qualities in such of them as singly fall under our senses, it is evident that some motion must be thence continued by our nerves or animal spirits, by some parts of our bodies, to the brains or the seat of sensation, there to produce in our minds the particular ideas we have of them. And since the extension, figure, number, and motion of bodies of an observable bigness, may be perceived at a distance by the sight, it is evident some singly imperceptible bodies must come from them to the eyes,

and thereby convey to the brain some motion which produces
these ideas which we have of them in us.

13. *How secondary.*—After the same manner that the ideas
of these original qualities are produced in us, we may conceive
that the ideas of secondary qualities are also produced, viz.,
by the operation of insensible particles on our senses. . . .
The different motions and figures, bulk and number of such particles, affecting the several organs of our senses, produce in
us those different sensations which we have from the colors
and smells of bodies; v.g., that a violet, by the impulse of
such insensible particles of matter of peculiar figures and
bulks, and in different degrees and modifications of their motions, causes the ideas of the blue color and sweet scent of
that flower to be produced in our minds.

14. What I have said concerning colors and smells may be
understood also of tastes and sounds, and other the like sensible qualities; which, whatever reality we by mistake attribute
to them, are in truth nothing in the objects themselves, but
powers to produce various sensations in us, and depend on those
primary qualities, viz., bulk, figure, texture, and motion of
parts, as I have said.

15. *Ideas of primary qualities are resemblances; of
secondary, not.*—From whence I think it is easy to draw this
observation, that the ideas of primary qualities of bodies are
resemblances of them, and their patterns do really exist in
the bodies themselves; but the ideas produced in us by these
secondary qualities have no resemblance of them at all. There
is nothing like our ideas existing in the bodies themselves.
They are, in the bodies we denominate from them, only a power
to produce those sensations in us: and what is sweet, blue, or
warm in idea, is but the certain bulk, figure, and motion of
the insensible parts in the bodies themselves, which we call
so.

16. Flame is denominated hot and light; snow, white and
cold; and manna, white and sweet, from the ideas they produce
in us. Which qualities are commonly thought to be the same in
those bodies that those ideas are in us, the one the perfect
resemblance of the other, as they are in a mirror; and it would
by most men be judged very extravagant, if one should say

otherwise. And yet he that will consider that the same fire that at one distance produces in us the sensation of warmth, does at a nearer approach produce in us the far different sensation of pain, ought to bethink himself what reason he has to say, that his idea of warmth which was produced in him by the fire, is actually in the fire, and his idea of pain which the same fire produced in him the same way is not in the fire. Why is whiteness and coldness in snow, and pain not, when it produces the one and the other idea in us, and can do neither, but by the bulk, figure, number, and motion of its solid parts?

17. The particular bulk, number, figure, and motion of the parts of fire or snow are really in them, whether any one's senses perceive them or no; and therefore they may be called *real qualities*, because they really exist in those bodies. But light, heat, whiteness, or coldness, are no more really in them than sickness or pain is in manna. Take away the sensation of them; let not the eyes see light or colors, nor the ears hear sounds; let the palate not taste, nor the nose smell; and all colors, tastes, odors, and sounds, as they are such particular ideas, vanish and cease, and are reduced to their causes, i.e., bulk, figure, and motion of parts.

22. I have, in what just goes before, been engaged in physical inquiries a little farther than perhaps I intended. But it being necessary to make the nature of sensation a little understood, and to make the difference between the *qualities* in bodies, and the *ideas* produced by them in the mind to be distinctly conceived, without which it were impossible to discourse intelligibly of them, I hope I shall be pardoned this little excursion into natural philosophy, it being necessary in our present inquiry to distinguish the *primary* and *real* qualities of bodies, which are always in them (viz., solidity, extension, figure, number, and motion or rest, and are sometimes perceived by us, viz., when the bodies they are in are big enough singly to be discerned), from those *secondary* and *imputed* qualities, which are but the powers of several combinations of those primary ones, when they operate without being distinctly discerned: whereby we also may come to know what ideas are, and what are not, resemblances of something really existing in the bodies we denominate from them.

23. *Three sorts of qualities in bodies*.—The qualities
then that are in bodies, rightly considered, are of three sorts:

First, the bulk, figure, number, situation, and motion or
rest of their solid parts. Those are in them, whether we perceive them or no; and when they are of that size that we can
discover them, we have by these an idea of the thing as it is
in itself, as is plain in artificial things. These I call
primary qualities.

Secondly, the power that is in any body, by reason of its
insensible primary qualities, to operate after a peculiar manner
on any of our senses, and thereby produce in *us* the different
ideas of several colors, sounds, smells, tastes, &c. These are
usually called *sensible qualities*.

Thirdly, the power that is in any body, by reason of the
particular constitution of its primary qualities, to make such
a change in the bulk, figure, texture, and motion of another
body, as to make it operate on our senses differently from what
it did before. Thus the sun has a power to make wax white, and
fire, to make lead fluid. These are usually called *powers*.

The first of these, as has been said, I think may be properly called real, original, or primary qualities, because they
are in the things themselves, whether they are perceived or no:
and upon their different modifications it is that the secondary
qualities depend.

The other two are only powers to act differently upon other
things, which powers result from the different modifications of
those primary qualities.

24. *The first are resemblances; the second thought resemblances, but are not; the third neither are, nor are thought so*.--
But though these two latter sorts of qualities are powers barely,
and nothing but powers, relating to several other bodies, and
resulting from the different modifications of the original qualities, yet they are generally otherwise thought of . . . V.g.,
the idea of heat or light which we receive by our eyes or touch
from the sun, are commonly thought real qualities existing in
the sun, and something more than mere powers in it. But when
we consider the sun in reference to wax, which it melts or

31

blanches, we look upon the whiteness and softness produced in
the wax, not as qualities in the sun, but effects produced by
powers in it: whereas, if rightly considered, these qualities
of light and warmth, which are perceptions in me when I am
warmed or enlightened by the sun, are no otherwise in the sun
than the changes made in the wax, when it is blanched or melted,
are in the sun. They are all of them equally powers in the
sun, depending on its primary qualities. . . .

OF OUR KNOWLEDGE OF THE EXISTENCE OF OTHER THINGS

1. *It is to be had only by sensation.*--The knowledge of
our own being we have by intuition.

The knowledge of the existence of any other thing we can
have only by sensation: for there being no necessary connexion
of real existence with any idea a man hath in his memory: no
particular man can know the existence of any other being, but
only when, by actual operating upon him, it makes itself perceived by him. For the having the idea of anything in our
mind no more proves the existence of that thing than the picture of a man evidences his being in the world, or the visions
of a dream make thereby a true history.

2. It is therefore the actual receiving of ideas from
without that gives us notice of the existence of other things,
and makes us know that something doth exist at that time without us which causes that idea in us, though perhaps we neither
know nor consider how it does it.

3. *This, though not so certain as demonstration, yet may
be called knowledge, and proves the existence of things without
us.*--The notice we have by **our senses** of the existing of things
without us, though it be not altogether so certain as our intuitive knowledge, or the deductions of our reason employed
about the clear abstract ideas of our own minds; yet it is an
assurance that deserves the name of *knowledge.*

4. *Because we cannot have them but by the inlet of the
senses.*--First, it is plain those perceptions are produced in
us by exterior causes affecting our senses, because those that
want the organs of any sense never can have the ideas belonging

32

to that sense produced in their minds. The organs themselves,
it is plain, do not produce them; for then the eyes of a man
in the dark would produce colors, and his nose smell roses in
the winter: but we see nobody gets the relish of a pine-apple
till he goes to the Indies where it is, and tastes it.

 5. *Because an idea from actual sensation and another
from memory are very distinct perceptions.*—Secondly, because
sometimes I find that I cannot avoid the having those ideas
produced in my mind. For though when my eyes are shut, or
windows fast, I can at pleasure recall to my mind the ideas
of light or the sun, which former sensations had lodged in my
memory; so I can at pleasure lay by that idea, and take into
my view that of the smell of a rose, or taste of sugar. But
if I turn my eyes at noon towards the sun, I cannot avoid the
ideas which the light or sun then produces in me. So that
there is a manifest difference between the ideas laid up in
my memory, and those which force themselves upon me, and I
cannot avoid having. And therefore it must needs be some exterior cause, and the brisk acting of some objects without me,
whose efficacy I cannot resist, that produces those ideas in
my mind, whether I will or no. Besides, there is nobody who
doth not perceive the difference in himself between contem-
plating the sun as he hath the idea of it in his memory, and
actually looking upon it: of which two, his perception is so
distinct, that few of his ideas are more distinguishable one
from another. And therefore he hath certain knowledge that
they are not both memory, or the actions of his mind, and fancies only within him; but that actual seeing hath a cause without.

 6. *Pleasure or pain, which accompanies actual sensation,
accompanies not the returning of those ideas without the external objects.*—Thirdly, add to this, that many of those ideas
are produced in us with pain, which afterwards we remember
without the least offence. Thus the pain of heat or cold, when
the idea of it is revived in our minds, gives us no disturbance;
which, when felt, was very troublesome, and is again, when actually repeated: which is occasioned by the disorder the external object causes in our bodies when applied to it. And
we remember the pain of hunger, thirst, or the headache, without any pain at all; which would either never disturb us, or
else constantly do it as often as we thought of it, were there

nothing more but ideas floating in our minds, and appearances
entertaining our fancies, without the real existence of things
affecting us from abroad. The same may be said of pleasure
accompanying several actual sensations. . . .

7. *Our senses assist one another's testimony of the
existence of outward things*.--Fourthly, our senses, in many
cases, bear witness to the truth of each other's report concerning the existence of sensible things without us. He that
sees a fire may, if he doubt whether it be anything more than
a bare fancy, feel it too, and be convinced by putting his hand
in it; which certainly could never be put into such exquisite
pain by a bare idea or phantom, unless that the pain be a fancy
too; which yet he cannot, when the burn is well, by raising the
idea of it, bring upon himself again.

9. *But reaches no farther than actual sensation*.--In fine,
then, when our senses do actually convey into our understandings
any idea, we cannot but be satisfied that there doth something
at that time really exist without us, which doth affect our
senses, and by them give notice of itself to our apprehensive
faculties, and actually produce that idea which we then perceive: and we cannot so far distrust their testimony as to doubt
that such collections of simple ideas as we have observed by
our senses to be united together, do really exist together. But
this knowledge extends as far as the present testimony of our
senses, employed about particular objects that do then affect
them, and no farther. For if I saw such a collection of simple
ideas as is wont to be called man, existing together one minute
since, and am now alone, I cannot be certain that the same man
exists now, since there is no necessary connexion of his existence a minute since with his existence now: by a thousand ways
he may cease to be, since I had the testimony of my senses for
his existence.

GEORGE BERKELEY

TO BE IS TO BE PERCEIVED

OF THE PRINCIPLES OF HUMAN KNOWLEDGE

    1. It is evident to anyone who take a survey of the ob-
jects of human knowledge, that they are either ideas (1) actually imprinted on the senses, or else such as are (2) perceived
by attending to the passions and operations of the mind, or
lastly (3) ideas formed by help of memory and imagination,
either compounding, dividing, or barely representing those originally perceived in the aforesaid ways. By sight I have the
ideas of lights and colors, with their several degrees and vari-
ations. By touch I perceive hard and soft, heat and cold, motion and resistance, and of all these more and less either as
to quantity or degree. Smelling furnishes me with odors, the
palate with tastes, and hearing conveys sounds to the mind in
all their variety of tone and composition. And as several of
these are observed to accompany each other, they come to be
marked by one name, and so to be reputed as one thing. Thus,
for example, a certain color, taste, smell, figure, and consistence, having been observed to go together, are accounted
one distinct thing, signified by the name 'apple'. Other collections of ideas constitute a stone, a tree, a book, and the
like sensible things; which, as they are pleasing or disagree-
able, excite the passions of love, hatred, joy, grief and so
forth.

    2. But besides all that endless variety of ideas or ob-
jects of knowledge, there is likewise something which knows or
perceives them, and exercises divers operations, as willing,

From George Berkeley, *A Treatise Concerning the Principles
of Human Knowledge*, first published in 1710, and *The Third
Dialogue Between Hylas and Philonous*, first published in 1713.

imagining, remembering, about them. This perceiving, active
being is what I call *mind, spirit, soul,* or *myself*. By which
words I do not denote any one of my ideas, but a thing entirely
distinct from them wherein they exist, or, which is the same
thing, whereby they are perceived; for the existence of an idea
consists in being perceived.

   3. That neither our thoughts, nor passions, nor ideas
formed by the imagination, exist without the mind, is what
everybody will allow. And it seems no less evident that the
the various sensations or ideas imprinted on the sense, however
blended or combined together (that is, whatever objects they
compose), cannot exist otherwise than in a mind perceiving them.
I think an intuitive knowledge may be obtained of this by anyone that shall attend to what is meant by the term 'exist' when
applied to sensible things. The table I write on I say exists--
that is, I see and feel it; and if I were out of my study I
should say it existed--meaning thereby that if I was in my
study I might perceive it, or that some other spirit actually
does perceive it. There was an odor, that is, it was smelt;
there was a sound, that is, it was heard; a color or figure,
and it was perceived by sight or touch. This is all that I
can understand by these and the like expressions. For as to
what is said of the absolute existence of unthinking things
without any relation to their being perceived that seems perfectly unintelligible. Their *esse* is *percipi*, nor is it possible they should have any existence out of the minds or thinking things which perceive them.

   4. It is indeed an opinion strangely prevailing amongst
men, that houses, mountains, rivers, and in a word all sensible
objects, have an existence, natural or real, distinct from
their being perceived by the understanding. But with how great
an assurance and acquiescence soever this principle may be
entertained in the world, yet whoever shall find in his heart
to call it in question may, if I mistake not, perceive it to
involve a manifest contradiction. For what are the foremention-
ed objects but the things we perceive by the sense? and what
do we perceive *besides our own ideas or sensations?* and is it
not plainly repugnant that any one of these, or any combination
of them, should exist unperceived?

6. Some truths there are so near and obvious to the mind that a man need only open his eyes to see them. Such I take this important one to be, to wit, that all the choir of heaven and furniture of the earth, in a word all those bodies which compose the mighty frame of the world, have not any subsistence without a mind, that their *being* is to be perceived or known; that consequently so long as they are not actually perceived by me, or do not exist in my mind or that of any other created spirit, they must either have no existence at all, or else subsist in the mind of some Eternal Spirit; it being perfectly unintelligible, and involving all the absurdity of abstraction, to attribute to any single part of them an existence independent of a spirit. To be convinced of which, the reader need only reflect and try to separate in his own thoughts the *being* of a sensible thing from its *being perceived.*

7. From what has been said it follows there is not any other substance than *spirit,* or that which perceives. But for the fuller proof of this point, let it be considered the sensible qualities are color, figure, motion, smell, taste, etc.—that is, the ideas perceived by sense. Now, for an idea to exist in an unperceiving thing is a manifest contradiction, for to have an idea is all one as to perceive; that therefore wherein color, figure, and the like qualities exist must perceive them; hence it is clear there can be no unthinking substance or *substratum* of those ideas.

8. But, say you, though the ideas themselves do not exist without the mind, yet there may be things *like* them, whereof they are copies or resemblances, which things exist without the mind in an unthinking substance. I answer, an idea can be like nothing but an idea; a color or figure can be like nothing but another color or figure. If we look but never so little into our thoughts, we shall find it impossible for us to conceive a likeness except only between our ideas. Again, I ask whether those supposed originals or external things, of which our ideas are the pictures or representations, be themselves perceivable or no? If they are, then they are ideas and we have gained our point; but if you say they are not, I appeal to anyone whether it be sense to assert a color is like something which is invisible; hard or soft, like something which is intangible; and so of the rest.

37

9. Some there are who make a distinction betwixt *primary* and *secondary* qualities. By the former they mean extension, figure, motion, rest, solidity or impenetrability, and number; by the latter they denote all other sensible qualities, as colors, sounds, tastes, and so forth. The ideas we have of these they acknowledge not to be the resemblances of anything existing without the mind, or unperceived, but they will have our ideas of the primary qualities to be patterns or images of things which exist without the mind, in an unthinking substance which they call *matter*. By *matter*, therefore, we are to understand an inert, senseless substance, in which extension, figure, and motion do actually subsist. But it is evident from what we have already shown, that extension, figure, and motion are only ideas existing in the mind, and that an idea can be like nothing but another idea, and that consequently neither they nor their archetypes can exist in an unperceiving substance. Hence, it is plain that the very notion of what is called *matter*, or *corporeal substance* involves a contradiction in it.

10. They who assert that figure, motion, and the rest of the primary or original qualities do exist without the mind in unthinking substances, do at the same time acknowledge that color, sounds, heat, cold, and such-like secondary qualities, do not; which they tell us are sensations existing in the mind alone, that depend on and are occasioned by the different size, texture, and motion of the minute particles of matter. This they take for an undoubted truth, which they can demonstrate beyond all exception. Now, if it be certain that those original qualities are inseparably united with the other sensible qualities, and not, even in thought, capable of being abstracted from them, it plainly follows that they exist only in the mind. But I desire anyone to reflect and try whether he can, by any abstraction of thought, conceive the extension and motion of a body without all other sensible qualities. For my own part, I see evidently that it is not in my power to frame an idea of a body extended and moving, but I must withal give it some color or other sensible quality which is acknowledged to exist only in the mind. In short, extension, figure, and motion, abstracted from all other qualities, are inconceivable. Where therefore the other sensible qualities are, there must these be also, to wit, in the mind and nowhere else.

14. I shall farther add that, after the same manner as modern philosophers prove certain sensible qualities to have no existence in matter, or without the mind, the same thing may be likewise proved of all other sensible qualities whatsoever. Thus, for instance, it is said that heat and cold are affections only of the mind, and not at all patterns of real beings, existing in the corporeal substances which excite them, for that the same body which appears cold to one hand seems warm to another. Now, why may we not as well argue that figure and extension are not patterns or resemblances of qualities existing in matter, because to the same eye at different stations, or eyes of a different texture at the same station, they appear various, and cannot therefore be the images of anything settled and determinate without the mind? Again, it is proved that sweetness is not really in the sapid thing, because the thing remaining unaltered the sweetness is changed into bitter, as in case of a fever or otherwise vitiated palate. Is it not as reasonable to say that motion is not without the mind, since if the succession of ideas in the mind become swifter, the motion, it is acknowledged, shall appear slower without any alteration in any external object?

15. In short, let anyone consider those arguments which are thought manifestly to prove that colors and tastes exist only in the mind, and he shall find they may with equal force be brought to prove the same thing of extension, figure, and motion—though it must be confessed this method of arguing does not so much prove that there is no extension or color in an outward object, as that we do not know by sense which is the true extension or color of the object. But the arguments foregoing plainly show it to be impossible that any color or extension at all, or other sensible quality whatsoever, should exist in an unthinking subject without the mind, or in truth, that there should be any such thing as an outward object.

18. But though it were possible that solid, figured, movable substances may exist without the mind, corresponding to the ideas we have of bodies, yet how is it possible for us to know this? Either we must know it by sense or by reason. As for our senses, by them we have the knowledge only of our sensations, ideas, or those things that are immediately perceived by sense, call them what you will; but they do not inform us that things exist without the mind, or unperceived,

like to those which are perceived. This the materialists
themselves acknowledge. It remains therefore that if we have
any knowledge at all of external things, it must be by reason,
inferring their existence from what is immediately perceived
by sense. But what reason can induce us to believe the existence of bodies without the mind, from what we perceive, since
the very patrons of matter themselves do not pretend there is
any necessary connection betwixt them and our ideas? I say
it is granted on all hands (and what happens in dreams, fren-
zies, and the like, puts it beyond dispute) that *it is possible we might be affected with all the ideas we have now,
though there were no bodies existing without, resembling them.*
Hence, it is evident the supposition of external bodies is not
necessary for the producing our ideas; since it is granted
they are produced sometimes, and might possibly be produced
always in the same order we see them in at present, without
their concurrence.

25. All our ideas, sensations, notions, or the things
which we perceive, by whatsoever names they may be distinguished, are visibly inactive: there is nothing of power or agency
included in them. So that one idea or object of thought cannot produce or make any alteration in another. To be satisfied of the truth of this, there is nothing else requisite
but a bare observation of our ideas. For, since they and
every part of them exist only in the mind, it follows that
there is nothing in them but what is perceived: but whoever
shall attend to his ideas, whether of sense or reflection, will
not perceive in them any power or activity; there is, therefore, no such thing contained in them. A little attention
will discover to us that the very being of an idea implies
passiveness and inertness in it, insomuch that it is impossible
for an idea to do anything, or, strictly speaking, to be the
cause of anything: neither can it be the resemblance or pattern of any active being, as is evident from Sec. 8. Whence
it plainly follows that extension, figure, and motion cannot
be the cause of our sensations. To say, therefore, that these
are the effects of powers resulting from the configuration,
number, motion, and size of corpuscles, must certainly be
false.

26. We perceive a continual succession of ideas, some
are anew excited, others are changed or totally disappear.

There is therefore some cause of these ideas, whereon they depend, and which produces and changes them. That this cause cannot be any quality or idea or combination of ideas, is clear from the preceding section. It must therefore be a substance; but it has been shewn that there is no corporeal or material substance: it remains therefore that the cause of ideas is an incorporeal active substance or Spirit.

27. A spirit is one simple, undivided, active being: as it perceives ideas it is called the *understanding,* and as it produces or otherwise operates about them it is called the *will.* Hence there can be no *idea* formed of a soul or spirit; for all ideas whatever, being passive and inert (*vide.*Sec.25), they cannot represent unto us, by way of image or likeness, that which acts. A little attention will make it plain to anyone, that to have an idea which shall be like that active principle of motion and change of ideas is absolutely impossible. Such is the nature of *spirit,* or that which acts, that it cannot be of itself perceived, but only by the effects which it produceth. If any man shall doubt of the truth of what is here delivered, let him but reflect and try if he can frame the idea of any power or active being, and whether he hath ideas of two principal powers, marked by the names *will* and *understanding,* distinct from each other as well as from a third idea of substance or being in general, with a relative notion of its supporting or being the subject of the aforesaid powers—which is signified by the name *soul* or *spirit.* This is what some hold; but, so far as I can see, the words *will, soul, spirit,* do not stand for different ideas, or, in truth, for any idea at all, but for something which is very different from ideas, and which, being an agent, cannot be like unto, or represented by, any idea whatsoever. Though it must be owned at the same time that we have some *notion* of soul, spirit, and the operations of the mind such as willing, loving, hating; inasmuch as we know or understand the meaning of these words.

28. I find I can excite ideas in my mind at pleasure, and vary and shift the scene as oft as I think fit. It is no more than willing, and straightway this or that idea arises in my fancy; and by the same power it is obliterated and makes way for another.

41

29. But, whatever power I may have over my own thoughts, I find the ideas actually perceived by sense have not a like dependence on my will. When in broad daylight I open my eyes, it is not in my power to choose whether I shall see or no, or to determine what particular objects shall present themselves to my view; and so likewise as to the hearing and other senses, the ideas imprinted on them are not creatures of my will. There is therefore some other will or spirit that produces them.

30. The ideas of sense are more strong, lively, and distinct than those of the imagination; they have likewise a steadiness, order, and coherence, and are not excited at random, as those which are the effects of human wills often are, but in a regular train or series, the admirable connection whereof sufficiently testifies the wisdom and benevolence of its Author. Now the set rules or established methods wherein the mind we depend on excites in us the ideas of sense, are called the *laws of nature*; and these we learn by experience, which teaches us that such and such ideas are attended with such and such other ideas, in the ordinary course of things.

33. The ideas imprinted on the senses by the Author of nature are called *real things*; and those excited in the imagination, being less regular, vivid, and constant, are more properly termed *ideas*, or *images* of *things*, which they copy and represent. But then our sensations, be they never so vivid and distinct, are nevertheless ideas, that is, they exist in the mind, or are perceived by it, as truly as the ideas of its own framing. The ideas of sense are allowed to have more reality in them, that is, to be more strong, orderly, and coherent than the creatures of the mind; but this is no argument that they exist without the mind. They are also less dependent on the spirit, or thinking substance which perceives them, in that they are excited by the will of another and more powerful spirit; yet still they are *ideas*, and certainly no idea, whether faint or strong, can exist otherwise than in a mind perceiving it.

34. Before we proceed any farther it is necessary we spend some time in answering objections which may probably be made against the principles we have hitherto laid down.

42

First, then, it will be objected that by the foregoing principles all that is real and substantial in nature is banished out of the world, and instead thereof a chimerical scheme of *ideas* takes place. All things that exist, exist only in the mind, that is, they are purely notional. What therefore becomes of the sun, moon, and stars? What must we think of houses, rivers, mountains, trees, stones; nay, even of our own bodies? Are all these but so many chimeras and illusions of the fancy? To all which, and whatever else of the same sort may be objected, I answer that by the principles premised we are not deprived of any one thing in nature. Whatever we see, feel, hear, or anywise conceive or understand remains as secure as ever, and is as real as ever. There is a *rerum natura,* and the distinction between realities and chimeras retains its full force. This is evident from Sec. 29, 30, and 33, where we have shewn what is meant by *real things* in opposition to *chimeras* or ideas of our own framing; but then they both equally exist in the mind, and in that sense they are alike *ideas.*

35. I do not argue against the existence of any one thing that we can apprehend either by sense or reflection. That the things I see with my eyes and touch with my hands do exist, really exist, I make not the least question. The only thing whose existence we deny is that which *philosophers* call matter or corporeal substance. And in doing of this there is no damage done to the rest of mankind, who, I dare say, will never miss it.

36. If any man thinks this detracts from the existence or reality of things, he is very far from understanding what hath been premised in the plainest terms I could think of. Take here an abstract of what has been said. There are spiritual substances, minds, or human souls, which will or excite ideas in themselves at pleasure; but these are faint, weak, and unsteady in respect of others they perceive by sense—which, being impressed upon them according to certain rules or laws of nature, speak themselves the effects of a mind more powerful and wise than human spirits. These latter are said to have more *reality* in them than the former; by which is meant that they are more affecting, orderly, and distinct, and that they are not fictions of the mind perceiving them. And in this sense the sun that I see by day is the real sun,

and that which I imagine by night is the idea of the former. In the sense here given of 'reality' it is evident that every vegetable, star, mineral, and in general each part of the mundane system, is as much as a real being by our principles as by any other. Whether others mean anything by the term 'reality' different from what I do, I entreat them to look into their own thoughts and see.

41. It will be objected that there is a great difference betwixt real fire for instance, and the idea of fire, betwixt dreaming or imagining oneself burnt, and actually being so: if you suspect it to be only the idea of fire which you see, do but put your hand into it and you will be convinced with a witness. This and the like may be urged in opposition to our tenets. To all which the answer is evident from what hath been already said; and I shall only add in this place, that if real fire be very different from the idea of fire, so also is the real pain that it occasions very different from the idea of the same pain, and yet nobody will pretend that real pain either is, or can possibly be, in an unperceiving thing, or without the mind, any more than its idea.

146. But though there be some things which convince us human agents are concerned in producing them; yet it is evident to everyone that those things which are called the works of nature, that is, the far greater part of the ideas or sensations perceived by us, are not produced by, or dependent on, the wills of men. There is therefore some other Spirit that causes them; since it is repugnant that they should subsist by themselves. (See Sec. 29) But if we attentively consider the constant regularity, order, and concatenation of natural things, the surprising magnificence, beauty, and perfection of the larger, and the exquisite contrivance of the smaller parts of creation, together with the exact harmony and correspondence of the whole, but above all the never enough admired laws of pain and pleasure, and the instincts or natural inclinations, appetites, and passions of animals; I say if we consider all these things, and at the same time attend to the meaning and import of the attributes One, Eternal, Infinitely Wise, Good, and Perfect, we shall clearly perceive that they belong to the aforesaid Spirit, "who works all in all," and "by whom all things consist."

THIRD DIALOGUE BETWEEN HYLAS AND PHILONOUS

Hyl. Since therefore you have no *idea* of the mind of
God, how can you conceive it possible that things should exist
in *His* mind? Or, if you can conceive the mind of God, without having an idea of it, why may not I be allowed to conceive
the existence of Matter, notwithstanding I have no idea of it?

Phil. As to your first question: I own I have properly
no *idea,* either of God or any other spirit; for these being
active, cannot be represented by things perfectly inert, as
our ideas are. I do nevertheless know that I, who am a spirit
or thinking substance, exist as certainly as I know my ideas
exist. Farther, I know what I mean by the terms *I* and *myself;*
and I know this immediately or intuitively, though I do not
perceive it as I perceive a triangle, a color, or a sound.
The Mind, Spirit, or Soul is that indivisible unextended thing
which thinks, acts, and perceives. I say *indivisible* because
unextended; and *unextended* because extended, figured, move-
able things are ideas; and that which perceives ideas, which
thinks and wills, is plainly itself no idea, nor like an idea.
Ideas are things inactive, and perceived. And Spirits a sort
of beings altogether different from them. I do not therefore
say my soul is an idea, or like an idea. However, taking the
word *idea* in a large sense, my soul may be said to furnish me
with an idea, that is, an image or likeness of God—though
indeed extremely inadequate. For, all the notion I have of
God is obtained by reflecting on my own soul, heightening its
powers, and removing its imperfections. I have, therefore,
though not an inactive idea, yet in *myself* some sort of an
active thinking image of the Deity. And, though I perceive
Him not by sense, yet I have a notion of Him, or know Him by
reflexion and reasoning. My own mind and my own ideas I have
an immediate knowledge of; and, by the help of these, do mediately apprehend the possibility of the existence of other
spirits and ideas. Farther, from my own being, and from the
dependency I find in myself and my ideas, I do, by an act of
reason, necessarily infer the existence of a God, and of all
created things in the mind of God. So much for your first
question. For the second: I suppose by this time you can
answer it yourself. For you neither perceive Matter objectively, as you do an inactive being or idea; nor know it, as

45

you do yourself, by a reflex act; neither do you mediately apprehend it by similitude of the one or the other; nor yet collect it by reasoning from that which you know immediately. All which makes the case of *matter* widely different from that of the *Deity*.

Hyl. You say your own soul supplies you with some sort of an idea or image of God. But, at the same time, you acknowledge you have, properly speaking, no *idea* of your own soul. You even affirm that spirits are a sort of beings altogether different from ideas. Consequently that no idea can be like a spirit. We have therefore no idea of any spirit. You admit nevertheless that there is spiritual Substance, although you have no idea of it; while you deny there can be such a thing as material Substance, because you have no notion or idea of it. Is this fair dealing? To act consistently, you must either admit Matter or reject Spirit. What say you to this?

Phil. I say, in the first place, that I do not deny the existence of material substance, merely because I have no notion of it, but because the notion of it is inconsistent; or, in other words, because it is repugnant that there should be a notion of it. Many things, for aught I know, may exist, whereof neither I nor any other man hath or can have any idea or notion whatsoever. But then those things must be possible, that is, nothing inconsistent must be included in their definition. I say, secondly, that, although we believe things to exist which we do not perceive, yet we may not believe that any particular thing exists, without some reason for such belief: but I have no reason for believing the existence of Matter. I have no immediate intuition thereof: neither can I immediately from my sensations, ideas, notions, actions, or passions, infer an unthinking, unperceiving, inactive Substance—either by probable deduction, or necessary consequence. Whereas the being of my Self, that is, my own soul, mind, or thinking principle, I evidently know by reflexion. You will forgive me if I repeat the same things in answer to the same objections. In the very notion or definition of *material substance,* there is included a manifest repugnance and inconsistency. But this cannot be said of the notion of Spirit. That ideas should exist in what doth not perceive, or be produced by what doth not act, is repugnant. But, it is no

46

repugnancy to say that a perceiving thing should be the subject of ideas, or an active thing the cause of them. It is
granted we have neither an immediate evidence nor a demonstrative knowledge of the existence of other finite spirits; but
it will not thence follow that such spirits are on a foot with
material substances: if to suppose the one be inconsistent,
and it be not inconsistent to suppose the other; if the one
can be inferred by no argument, and there is a probability for
the other; if we see signs and effects indicating distinct
finite agents like ourselves, and see no sign or symptom whatever that leads to a rational belief of Matter. I say, lastly,
that I have a notion of Spirit, though I have not, strictly
speaking, an idea of it. I do not perceive it as an idea, or
by means of an idea, but know it by reflexion.

Hyl. Notwithstanding all you have said, to me it seems
that, according to your own way of thinking, and in consequence
of your own principles, it should follow that *you* are only a
system of floating ideas, without any substance to support
them. Words are not to be used without a meaning. And, as
there is no more meaning in *spiritual substance* than in *material substance,* the one is to be exploded as well as the other.

Phil. How often must I repeat, that I know or am conscious of my own being; and that *I myself* am not my ideas, but
somewhat else, a thinking, active principle that perceives,
knows, wills, and operates about ideas. I know that I, one
and the same self, perceive both colors and sounds: that a
color cannot perceive a sound, nor a sound a color: that I am
therefore one individual principle, distinct from color and
sound; and, for the same reason, from all other sensible
things and inert ideas. But, I am not in like manner conscious either of the existence or essence of Matter. On the
contrary, I know that nothing inconsistent can exist, and
that the existence of Matter implies an inconsistency. Farther,
I know what I mean when I affirm that there is a spiritual
substance or support of ideas, that is, that a spirit knows
and perceives ideas. But, I do not know what is meant when
it is said that an unperceiving substance hath inherent in it
and supports either ideas or the archetypes of ideas. There
is therefore upon the whole no parity of case between Spirit
and Matter.

PLATO

AN ALLEGORY: THE CAVE OF IGNORANCE

We speak of many beautiful things and many good things, and we say that they are so and so define them in speech, /said Socrates7. -- We do, /said Glaucon7.

And Beauty itself and Goodness itself, and so with all the things which we then classed as many; we now class them again according to one Form of each, which is one and which we in each case call that which is. -- That is so.

And we say that the many things are the objects of sight but not of thought, while the Forms are the objects of thought but not of sight. -- Altogether true.

With what part of ourselves do we see the objects that are seen? -- With our sight.

And so things heard are heard by our hearing, and all that is perceived is perceived by our other senses? -- Quite so.

. . .

You know, I said, that when one turns one's eyes to those objects of which the colours are no longer in the light of day but in the dimness of the night, the eyes are dimmed and seem nearly blind, as if clear vision was no longer in them. -- Quite so.

From *Plato's REPUBLIC*, translated by G. M. A. Grube, c 1974, Hackett Publishing Company, Inc., Indianapolis, Indiana, 46205. Reprinted by permission of the publisher.

Yet whenever one's eyes are turned upon objects bright-
ened by sunshine, they see clearly, and clear vision appears
in those very same eyes? -- Yes indeed.

So too understand the eye of the soul: whenever it is
fixed upon that upon which truth and reality shine, it under-
stands and knows and seems to have intelligence, but whenever
it is fixed upon what is mixed with darkness--that which is
subject to birth and destruction--it opines and is dimmed,
changes its opinions this way and that, and seems to have no
intelligence. -- That is so.

. . .

Understand then, I said, that, as we say, there are those
two, one reigning over the intelligible kind and realm, the
other over the visible (not to say heaven, that I may not appear to play the sophist about the name). So you have two
kinds, the visible and the intelligible. -- Right.

It is like a line divided into two unequal parts, and
then divide each section in the same ratio, that is, the section of the visible and that of the intelligible. You will
then have sections related to each other in proposition to
their clarity and obscurity. . . . -- I understand.

. . .

. . . There are four such processes in the soul, corresponding to the four sections of our line: understanding for
the highest, reasoning for the second; give the name of opinion
to the third, and imagination to the last. Place these in the
due terms of a proportion and consider that each has as much
clarity as the content of its particular section shares in
truth. -- I understand, and I agree and arrange them as you
say.

. . .

Next, I said, compare the effect of education and the
lack of it upon our human nature to a situation like this:
imagine men to be living in an underground cave-like dwelling
place, which has a way up to the light along its whole width,

49

but the entrance is a long way up. The men have been there from childhood, with their neck and legs in fetters, so that they remain in the same place and can only see ahead of them, as their bonds prevent them turning their heads. Light is provided by a fire burning some way behind and above them. Between the fire and the prisoners, some way behind them and on a higher ground, there is a path across the cave and along this a low wall has been built, like the screen at a puppet show in front of the performers who show their puppets above it. -- I see it.

See then also men carrying along that wall, so that they overtop it, all kinds of artifacts, statues of men, reproductions of other animals in stone or wood fashioned in all sorts of ways, and, as is likely, some of the carriers are talking while others are silent. -- This is a strange picture, and strange prisoners.

They are like us, I said. Do you think, in the first place, that such men could see anything of themselves and each other except the shadows which the fire casts upon the wall of the cave in front of them? -- How could they, if they have to keep their heads still throughout life?

And is not the same true of the objects carried along the wall? -- Quite.

If they could converse with one another, do you not think that they would consider these shadows to be the real things?-- Necessarily.

What if their prison had an echo which reached them from in front of them? Whenever one of the carriers passing behind the wall spoke, would they not think that it was the shadow passing in front of them which was talking? Do you agree? -- By Zeus I do.

Altogether then, I said, such men would believe the truth to be nothing else than the shadows of the artifacts? -- They must believe that.

Consider then what deliverance from their bonds and the curing of their ignorance would be if something like this naturally happened to them. Whenever one of them was freed, had to stand up suddenly, turn his head, walk, and look up toward the light, doing all that would give him pain, the flash of the fire would make it impossible for him to see the objects of which he had earlier seen the shadows. What do you think he would say if he was told that what he saw then was foolishness, that he was now somewhat closer to reality and turned to things that existed more fully, that he saw more correctly? If one then pointed to each of the objects passing by, asked him what each was, and forced him to answer, do you not think he would be at a loss and believe that the things which he saw earlier were truer than the things now pointed out to him? -- Much truer.

If one then compelled him to look at the fire itself, his eyes would hurt, he would turn aound and flee toward those things which he could see, and think that they were in fact clearer than those now shown to him. -- Quite so.

And if one were to drag him thence by force up the rough and steep path, and did not let him go before he was dragged into the sunlight, would he not be in physical pain and angry as he was dragged along? When he came into the light, with the sunlight filling his eyes, he would not be able to see a single one of the things which are now said to be true. -- Not at once, certainly.

I think he would need time to get adjusted before he could see things in the world above; at first he would see shadows most easily, then reflections of men and other things in water, then the things themselves. After this he would see objects in the sky and the sky itself more easily at night, the light of the stars and the moon more easily than the sun and the light of the sun during the day. -- Of course.

Then, at last, he would be able to see the sun, not images of it in the water or in some alien place, but the sun itself in its own place, and be able to contemplate it. -- That must be so.

After this he would reflect that it is the sun which provides the seasons and the years, which governs everything in the visible world, and is also in some way the cause of those other things which he used to see. -- Clearly that would be the next stage.

What then? As he reminds himself of his first dwelling place, of the wisdom there and of his fellow prisoners, would he not reckon himself happy for the change, and pity them? -- Surely.

And if the men below had praise and honours from each other, and prizes for the man who saw most clearly the shadows that passed before them, and who could best remember which usually came earlier and which later, and which came together and thus could most ably prophesy the future, do you think our man would desire those rewards and envy those who were honoured and held power among the prisoners, or would he feel, as Homer put it, that he certainly wished to be "serf to another man without possessions upon the earth" and go through any suffering, rather than share their opinions and live as they do? -- Quite so, he said, I think he would rather suffer anything.

Reflect on this too, I said. If this man went down into the cave again and sat down in the same seat, would his eyes not be filled with darkness, coming suddenly out of the sunlight? -- They certainly would.

And if he had to contend again with those who had remained prisoners in recognizing those shadows while his sight was affected and his eyes had not settled down--and the time for this adjustment would not be short--would he not be ridiculed? Would it not be said that he had returned from his upward journey with his eyesight spoiled, and that it was not worthwhile even to attempt to travel upward? As for the man who tried to free them and lead them upward, if they could somehow lay their hands on him and kill him, they would do so. -- They certainly would.

This whole image, my dear Glaucon, I said, must be related to what we said before. The realm of the visible should be compared to the prison dwelling, and the fire inside it to the power of the sun. If you interpret the upward journey and the contemplation of things above as the upward journey of the soul to the intelligible realm, you will grasp what I surmise

since you were keen to hear it. Whether it is true or not
only the god knows, but this is how I see it. . .

CHAPTER TWO

INDUCTIVE REASONING

THE PROBLEM OF INDUCTION

> *What does this mean?—"The certainty that the*
> *fire will burn me is based on induction." Does that*
> *mean that I argue to myself: "Fire has always burned*
> *me, so it will happen now too?" Or is the previous*
> *experience the cause of my certainty, not its ground?*
> *We expect this, and are surprised at that. But*
> *the chain of reasons has an end.*
> —Ludwig Wittgenstein

Suppose a player hits a baseball into the air toward left field. Is there any good reason to think that the ball upon reaching its apex will fall towards the ground? Any ordinary person would unhesitantly answer this question in the affirmative. He would probably claim there is an excellent reason to think so, namely, that whenever in the past a baseball has been hit in the air it has subsequently come back down. He might go further, counting as evidence the entirety of his past experiences with things being tossed in the air and their eventual return to the ground (excepting, of course, special cases such as rockets). In fact, he may go so far as to include as evidence all observed confirmations of the law of gravity.

The reasoning process being utilized in this example is called *induction*. It is a case of referring to past experiences in order to justify a belief about, or make an inference about, a future happening. The logical principle involved in this type of reasoning, what we will call the *principle of induction,* can be expressed as follows: "When a thing of a certain sort A has been found to be associated with a thing

of a certain other sort B, and has never been found dissoci-
ated from a thing of the sort B, the greater the number of
cases in which A and B have been associated, the greater is
the probability that they will be associated in a fresh case
in which one of them is known to be present."[1]

As an extension of this principle it follows that, other
conditions being equal, a sufficient number of instances of
association will raise the probability to near certainty that
likewise in the next instance A will be associated with B.
Nevertheless, though the probability may become extremely
high, it is evident that inductive conclusions can never attain the status of absolute certainty. Notice that this in
itself does not count as an objection against the principle,
since probability is all that we should expect from inductive
reasoning; in other words, if induction yields highly probable results, then it has successfully fulfilled its purpose.

This may all seem simple enough and readily acceptable.
But there have been philosophers--such as Hume and Russell--
who have disputed the legitimacy of the inductive principle.
Their arguments are worth considering, because if the inductive principle cannot be satisfactorily justified this would
have severe consequences regarding our trust in the general
principles of science--e.g. the law of gravity, the laws of
motion, and the principle that every event has a cause--as
well as the reliability of our most common beliefs in ordinary life.

As a matter of preparation an important distinction needs
to be clarified. It is clear from experience that the frequent repetition of some uniform association of certain types
of events creates in us an expectation for a similar association in the future. After having eaten excellent t-bone steak
at a particular restaurant every Monday evening for two years,
we come to expect the steak to be excellent the next time
also. If a mother has telephoned her son every Sunday night
at 11:00 o'clock for the last ten years without fail, the son

---

[1]This is Bertrand Russell's statement of the principle;
The Problems of Philosophy (New York: Oxford University Press,
1959), p. 66.

psychologically comes to expect the call each Sunday. Animals are no different. As Russell notes, a horse which has been often driven along a certain road resists any attempt to drive him in another direction, and chickens expect food when they see the person who usually feeds them. But as we all know, these rather crude expectations are liable to be misleading. The steak unexpectedly turns out to be tough, one Sunday night the mother does not call, and the man who has fed the chicken every day of its life at last wrings its neck instead.

The crucial distinction to be drawn is between the mere *having of expectations,* which is purely a psychological matter explainable in terms of habitual repetitions of uniformity, and the *having of rational grounds* for such expectations, which is a logical matter. It is strictly this latter concern which poses the problem for induction. The real question is not whether we have expectations based on past repetitions, rather, assuming that certain uniformities have always held in the past, whether we have rational grounds for thinking they will hold in the future.

For purposes of discussion the problem of induction can be formulated by raising two questions:

(1) Assuming that we have observed *n* positive instances of an association, and that we have not observed a single negative instance (where *n* is a large number), have we any good reason to think that the *n +* 1st instance probably will also be positive?

(2) Is there any number *n* of observed positive instances of an association which affords sufficient evidence that the *n +* 1st instance probably will also be positive?

The inductive sceptic asserts that both questions must be answered negatively. If the sceptic is correct, it follows that there is neither sufficient evidence nor good reason for believing that the baseball will come down, that the sun will rise tomorrow, that water will quench our thirst and not poison us, or for any of the other conscious or unconscious expectations that govern our daily lives.

Three types of arguments have been brought forth against induction.

A. Examples can be found where a large number of positive instances and not a single negative instance of a certain association have been observed and where the next instance nevertheless turned out to be negative. A man has performed a hazardous trapeze act over a thousand times in his life and has never fallen once—until today! An expensive wristwatch has kept perfect time for fifteen years without exception, yet today it was five minutes slow. The point is that in spite of frequent repetitions of a certain phenomenon there sometimes is a negative instance at last. And this just might happen the next time a baseball is hit in the air, or the next time we turn the faucet and expect water to come, or maybe the next time we strike the cue ball and expect it to knock the eight ball into the side pocket: who knows?—Maybe the cue ball will float to the ceiling and start singing!

The obvious reply, however, to this type of argument is to show that the falsehood of an inductive inference is no proof against the principle itself. An inference may indeed be quite reasonable and yet turn out to be false. Probability is always relative to a set of past observations. New observations may gravely alter the probability. Citing an example from Russell, suppose a person had seen a great many white swans. He might inductively infer that all swans are white. On the basis of the induction principle this is a perfectly reasonable argument. Neither the strength of the argument nor the legitimacy of the principle is disproven (or even reduced) by the fact that the next swan he sees is black. The argument was not meant to be absolutely certain, only probable; even though something is highly probable it might well turn out to be false. Not that the principle itself is false, only that the original inference is now rendered false on the basis of the new observation, the new piece of data. In short, the falsehood of a particular inductive inference in no way discredits the principle itself.

B. The number of conditions affecting the occurrence of a given event is infinite or at least too large to be directly observed by an individual or even a group of individuals. Thus we can never be in a position to sufficiently warrant an

60

inference regarding a future occurrence of the event. Who
knows, maybe a determining element for the sun rising in the
east is the activity of a genie that lives on Mars? None of
us can be sure there is no such genie who, possibly to play
a joke on us, will prevent the sun from rising tomorrow.
Similarly, we can never be sure that such a genie will not
make grape juice come out of the water faucet, or make the
baseball fly away and never come down. Hence inductive reasoning about the future is nothing but unwarranted speculation.

In response to such an objection it may readily be admitted that finite human beings are indeed incapable of knowing everything, and that in particular they are incapable of
knowing all the conditions affecting the occurrence of given
events. But the reliability of inductive reasoning does not
depend on having such absolute knowledge. In fact, it is
precisely because we cannot know everything that we must rely
on some principle such as induction. Because we cannot *be
sure* there is no mysterious genie controlling the way things
happen, we must rely totally on that which is available to
us—i.e. past observations.

C. Any attempt to justify induction by drawing upon past
experience involves the logical fallacy known as *begging the
question*.[1] Defenders of common sense argue that induction can
be justified on grounds that it works, as evidenced by the
impressive achievements of modern science and by how efficient-
ly we get along in everyday life using the inductive principle.
But what can it mean to say that induction *works*? If it means
only that induction has led to correct conclusions in the
past, then it is obviously true but totally irrelevant. What
is at stake is whether it will yield correct conclusions in
the future. The question is: assuming that a large number of
observed instances are positive, is that sufficient reason to
think that the next instance—not yet observed—probably will
also be positive? On the other hand, if the commonsense claim
means that not only has induction proven successful in the
past but it will continue to be successful in the future, then

---

[1]An argument is said to beg the question if one of the
steps used to derive the conclusion is explicitly or implic-
itly an equivalent statement of the conclusion itself.

the statement simply begs the question. How can we ever reason about the future without recourse to the inductive principle?—But that is the very principle we are trying to justify! It is circular reasoning. Russell makes the point rather uniquely: "We have experience of past futures, but not of future futures, and the question is: will future futures resemble past futures? This question is not to be answered by an argument which starts from past futures alone."[1]

It is this third type of argument that has proven the most difficult to overcome. Let us consider a hypothetical situation. Suppose in 1950 a scientist declares that with respect to baseballs being hit into the air and falling to the ground, the future will resemble the past. To substantiate his claim, the scientist spends the next twenty years of his life gathering data, watching baseball games, hitting pop flies to Little League teams, etc. Wouldn't all this data count as evidence to document the scientific claim that in the future baseballs will (probably) follow the patterns of the past? In 1950, 1970 was the future, and indeed the patterns of 1970 were the same as in 1950. The sceptic is quick to point out, however, that although 1970 *used to be* the future it is *now the past,* which means that the totality of the gathered data over the twenty-year span proves merely that *in the past* baseballs have followed a uniform pattern—but what does the past have to do with reasoning about the future? Even after twenty years of empirical observation, it appears that our hypothetical scientist is left with the same problem with which he began, and is not even one iota closer to an answer.

It might be objected that the sceptic's argument depends on confusing the meaning of 'future'.[2] Two senses of the word may be discriminated, what we will designate as future-1 and future-2. In the ordinary sense of the term (future-1), future simply means some period of time which has to the past

---

[1]Bertrand Russell, *The Problems of Philosophy* (New York: Oxford University Press, 1959), p. 65.

[2]Cf. Frederick Will, "Will the Future Be Like the Past?" *Mind,* vol. LVI (1947).

62

and present the relation of happening after. Herein the term refers to events which have not occurred, things which do not exist, with the implication that through the passing of time such events and things may actually come into being. The year 2000 is definitely in the future, though we can conceive it as eventually revealing itself to us as it comes into being.

There is another sense, future-2, in which the future is conceived as a time which is always ahead of the present, a time which by definition never comes into being, no matter how far the present moves forward. It's analogous to the kind of verbal trick which children often play upon one another in fun. Joey asks Timmy what he is going to do tomorrow. Timmy replies that he is going to go swimming, whereupon Joey exclaims "You can't do that." Why not, asks Timmy? To which Joey replies that tomorrow never comes. When tomorrow comes, it won't be tomorrow; it will be today! Likewise, the future never comes: when it comes, it won't be the future—it will be the present and will become the past.

When sceptics deny that observance of past uniformities counts as evidence regarding future occurrences, and when philosophers such as Russell introduce expressions like 'future future' and 'past future', they seem to have in mind something like the sense of future-2. It may be the case that the entire sceptical argument reduces to nothing more than a verbal trick. If so, perhaps the sceptic should be taken no more seriously than we do children playing their verbal games.

The more legitimate meaning of future, it would seem, is in the sense of future-1. No government diplomat wastes a moment worrying about the kind of future wars, future-2 wars, which by definition can never happen. But he most definitely might worry about a future war which conceivably can occur, can come into being at some point in time. Likewise, it may be argued, when in science and everyday life we employ inductive reasoning about the future, the only pertinent meaning is that of future-1. Hence, if we utilize the sense of future-1, then it appears that we have plenty of evidence for the claim that the future will resemble the past in regard to certain uniformities. The future is constantly unfolding itself for inspection, and every new experience which accords

with the past is just one more piece of evidence confirming
the inductive conclusion that the future will resemble the
past.

While distinguishing the two senses of 'future' seems to
be the most effective way to answer the inductive sceptic
regarding the problem of circularity and begging the question,
even here the sceptic has a quick reply: what justification
is there for grounding the inductive principle in the sense
of future-1 instead of future-2? The only answer seems to be,
because it is more useful, it works better! And why does it
work better? --Because it allows for reasoning about the future on the basis of the past! Says the sceptic, however,
isn't this merely to beg the question, but one step removed?
It is illegitimate to justify induction by utilizing the meaning of future-1, and then turn around and argue for the use
of future-1 on grounds that it justifies induction.

Where does this leave us? Of the numerous 'solutions'
to the problem of induction which have been proposed at one
time or another, all turn out, on reflection, to be vulnerable
to critical objections. If there is something wrong with the
sceptical argument of type C (above), as yet no one has provided a convincing account of what it is that is wrong. It
may be that inductive scepticism is something we must learn
to live with, no matter how much it may offend our commonsense
intuitions. It may be that our only recourse is to accept the
inductive principle as an article of faith, as a mere assumption for the utility of science and everyday human conduct.
Even Hume himself admitted that he was not able to adhere to
his sceptical position outside his study. Like the rest of
us, he allowed himself to be guided in his practical affairs
by what he called his natural beliefs, but he did not claim
that this was rationally justifiable.

DAVID HUME

SCEPTICAL DOUBTS CONCERNING THE OPERATIONS OF THE UNDERSTANDING

All the objects of human reason or inquiry may naturally
be divided into two kinds, to wit, "Relations of Ideas," and
"Matters of Fact." Of the first kind are the sciences of Geometry, Algebra, and Arithmetic, and, in short, every affirmation which is either intuitively or demonstratively certain.
*That the square of the hypotenuse is equal to the square of
the two sides* is a proposition which expresses a relation between these figures. *That three times five is equal to the
half of thirty* expresses a relation between these numbers.
Propositions of this kind are discoverable by the mere operation of thought, without dependence on what is anywhere existent in the universe. Though there never were a circle or
triangle in nature, the truths demonstrated by Euclid would
forever retain their certainty and evidence.

Matters of fact, which are the second objects of human
reason, are not ascertained in the same manner, nor is our
evidence of their truth, however great, of a like nature with
the foregoing. The contrary of every matter of fact is still
possible, because it can never imply a contradiction and is
conceived by the mind with the same facility and distinctness
as if ever so conformable to reality. *That the sun will not
rise tomorrow* is no less intelligible a proposition and implies
no more contradiction than the affirmation *that it will rise.*
We should in vain, therefore, attempt to demonstrate its falsehood. Were it demonstratively false, it would imply a contradiction and could never be distinctly conceived by the mind.

It may, therefore, be a subject worthy of curiosity to

From David Hume, *An Inquiry Concerning Human Understanding,* Section IV, first published in 1748.

inquire what is the nature of that evidence which assures us
of any real existence and matter of fact beyond the present
testimony of our senses or the records of our memory. . . .

   All reasonings concerning matter of fact seem to be
founded on the relation of *cause* and *effect.* By means of
that relation alone we can go beyond the evidence of our memory and senses. If you were to ask a man why he believes any
matter of fact which is absent, for instance, that his friend
is in the country or in France, he would give you a reason,
and this reason would be some other fact: as a letter received
from him or the knowledge of his former resolutions and prom-
ises. A man finding a watch or any other machine in a desert
island would conclude that there had once been men on that
island. All our reasonings concerning fact are of the same
nature. And here it is constantly supposed that there is a
connection between the present fact and that which is inferred
from it. Were there nothing to bind them together, the inference would be entirely precarious. The hearing of an articulate voice and rational discourse in the dark assures us
of the presence of some person. Why? Because these are the
effects of the human make and fabric; and closely connected
with it. If we anatomize all the other reasonings of this
nature, we shall find that they are founded on the relation
of cause and effect, and that this relation is either near or
remote, direct or collateral. Heat and light are collateral
effects of fire, and the one effect may justly be inferred
from the other.

                              • • •

   But we have not yet attained any tolerable satisfaction
with regard to the question first proposed. Each solution
still gives rise to a new question as difficult as the foregoing and leads us on to further inquiries. When it is asked,
*What is the nature of all our reasonings concerning matter of
fact?* the proper answer seems to be, That they are founded
on the relation of cause and effect. When again it is asked,
*What is the foundation of all our reasonings and conclusions
concerning that relation?* it may be replied in one word,
experience. But if we still carry on our sifting humor and
ask, *What is the foundation of all conclusions from experience?*
this implies a new question which may be of more difficult

solution and explication. . . .

   I shall content myself in this section with an easy task
and shall pretend only to give a negative answer to the question here proposed. I say, then, that even after we have experience of the operations of cause and effect, our conclusions
from that experience are *not* founded on reasoning or any process of the understanding. This answer we must endeavor both
to explain and to defend.

   It must certainly be allowed that nature has kept us at
a great distance from all her secrets and has afforded us only
the knowledge of a few superficial qualities of objects, while
she conceals from us those powers and principles on which the
influence of these objects entirely depends. Our senses inform us of the color, weight, and consistency of bread, but
neither sense nor reason can ever inform us of those qualities
which fit it for the nourishment and support of the human body.
Sight or feeling conveys an idea of the actual motion of bodies,
but as to that wonderful force or power which would carry on
a moving body forever in a continued change of place, and which
bodies never lose but by communicating it to others, of this
we cannot form the most distant conception. But notwithstanding this ignorance of natural powers and principles, we always
presume when we see like sensible qualities that they have
like secret powers, and expect that effects similar to those
which we have experienced will follow from them. If a body of
like color and consistency with that bread which we have formerly eaten be presented to us, we make no scruple of repeat-
ing the experiment and foresee with certainty like nourishment
and support. Now this is a process of the mind or thought of
which I would willingly know the foundation. It is allowed
on all hands that there is no known connection between the
sensible qualities and the secret powers, and, consequently,
that the mind is not led to form such a conclusion concerning
their constant and regular conjunction by anything which it
knows of their nature. As to past *experience,* it can be allowed to give *direct* and *certain* information of those precise
objects only, and that precise period of time which fell under
its cognizance: But why this experience should be extended to
future times and to other objects which, for aught we know,
may be only in appearance similar, this is the main question

on which I would insist. The bread which I formerly ate
nourished me; that is, a body of such sensible qualities was,
at that time, endued with such secret powers. But does it
follow that other bread must also nourish me at another time,
and that like sensible qualities must always be attended with
like secret powers? The consequence seems nowise necessary.
At least, it must be acknowledged that there is here a consequence drawn by the mind that there is a certain step taken,
a process of thought, and an inference which wants to be explained. These two propositions are far from being the same:
*I have found that such an object has always been attended with
such an effect,* and *I foresee that other objects which are in
appearance similar will be attended with similar effects.* I
shall allow, if you please, that the one proposition may justly
be inferred from the other: I know, in fact, that it always is
inferred. But if you insist that the inference is made by a
chain of reasoning, I desire you to produce that reasoning.
The connection between these propositions is not intuitive.
There is required a medium which may enable the mind to draw
such an inference, if indeed it be drawn by reasoning and argument. What that medium is I must confess passes my compre-
hension; and it is incumbent on those to produce it who assert
that it really exists and is the original of all our conclusions concerning matter of fact.

   All reasonings may be divided into two kinds, namely,
demonstrative reasoning, or that concerning relations of ideas,
and moral reasoning, or that concerning matter of fact and
existence. That there are no demonstrative arguments in the
case seems evident, since it implies no contradiction that the
course of nature may change and that an object, seemingly like
those which we have experienced, may be attended with different
or contrary effects. May I not clearly and distinctly conceive
that a body, falling from the clouds and which in all other
respects resembles snow, has yet the taste of salt or feeling
of fire? Is there any more intelligible proposition than to
affirm that all the trees will flourish in December and Jan-
uary, and will decay in May and June? Now, whatever is intelligible and can be distinctly conceived implies no contradiction and can never be proved false by any demonstrative argument or abstract reasoning *a priori.*

If we be, therefore, engaged by arguments to put trust in past experience and make it the standard of our future judgment, these arguments must be probable only, or such as regard matter of fact and real existence, according to the division above mentioned. But that there is no argument of this kind must appear if our explication of that species of reasoning be admitted as solid and satisfactory. We have said that all arguments concerning existence are founded on the relation of cause and effect, that our knowledge of that relation is derived entirely from experience, and that all our experimental conclusions proceed upon the supposition that the future will be conformable to the past. To endeavor, therefore, the proof of this last supposition by probable arguments, or arguments regarding existence, must be evidently going in a circle and taking that for granted which is the very point in question.

In reality, all arguments from experience are founded on the similarity which we discover among natural objects, and by which we are induced to expect effects similar to those which we have found to follow from such objects. And though none but a fool or madman will ever pretend to dispute the authority of experience or to reject that great guide of human life, it may surely be allowed a philosopher to have so much curiosity at least as to examine the principle of human nature which gives this mighty authority to experience and makes us draw advantage from that similarity which nature has placed among different objects. From causes which appear similar, we expect similar effects. This is the sum of all our experimental conclusions. Now it seems evident that, if this conclusion were formed by reason, it would be as perfect at first, and upon one instance, as after ever so long a course of experience; but the case is far otherwise. Nothing so like as eggs, yet no one, on account of this appearing similarity, expects the same taste and relish in all of them. It is only after a long course of uniform experiments in any kind that we attain a firm reliance and security with regard to a particular event. Now, where is that process of reasoning which, from one instance, draws a conclusion so different from that which it infers from a hundred instances that are nowise different from that single one? This question I propose as much for the sake of information as with an intention of raising

difficulties. I cannot find, I cannot imagine any such reasoning. But I keep my mind still open to instruction if anyone will vouchsafe to bestow it on me.

   . . . When a new object endowed with similar sensible
qualities is produced, we expect similar powers and forces,
and look for a like effect. From a body of like color and
consistency with bread, we expect like nourishment and support. But this surely is a step or progress of the mind which
wants to be explained. When a man says, *I have found, in all
past instances, such sensible qualities, conjoined with such
secret powers,* and when he says, *similar sensible qualities
will always be conjoined with similar secret powers,* he is not
guilty of a tautology, nor are these propositions in any respect the same. You say that the one proposition is an inference from the other;but you must confess that the inference is
not intuitive, neither is it demonstrative. Of what nature is
it then? To say it is experimental is begging the question.
For all inferences from experience suppose, as their foundation, that the future will resemble the past and that similar
powers will be conjoined with similar sensible qualities. If
there be any suspicion that the course of nature may change,
and that the past may be no rule for the future, all experience
becomes useless and can give rise to no inference or conclusion. It is impossible, therefore, that any arguments from
experience can prove this resemblance of the past to the future, since all these arguments are founded on the supposition
of that resemblance. Let the course of things be allowed
hitherto ever so regular, that alone, without some new argument or inference, proves not that for the future it will continue so. In vain do you pretend to have learned the nature
of bodies from your experience. Their secret nature, and consequently all their effects and influence, may change without
any change in their sensible qualities. This happens sometimes,
and with regard to some objects. Why may it not happen always,
and with regard to all objects? What logic, what process of
argument secures you against this supposition? My practice,
you say, refutes my doubts. But you mistake the purport of my
question. As an agent, I am quite satisfied in the point; but
as a philosopher who has some share of curiosity, I will not
say scepticism, I want to learn the foundation of this inference. No reading, no inquiry has yet been able to remove my

70

difficulty or give me satisfaction in a matter of such importance. Can I do better than propose the difficulty to the
public, even though, perhaps, I have small hopes of obtaining
a solution? We shall at least, by this means, be sensible of
our ignorance, if we do not augment our knowledge.

It is certain that the most ignorant and stupid peasants,
nay infants, nay even brute beasts, improve by experience and
learn the qualities of natural objects by observing the effects
which result from them. When a child has felt the sensation
of pain from touching the flame of a candle, he will be careful not to put his hand near any candle, but will expect a
similar effect from a cause which is similar in its sensible
qualities and appearance. If you assert, therefore, that the
understanding of the child is led into this conclusion by any
process of argument or ratiocination, I may justly require
you to produce that argument, nor have you any pretense to
refuse so equitable a demand. You cannot say that the argument is abstruse and may possibly escape your inquiry, since
you confess that it is obvious to the capacity of a mere in-
fant. If you hesitate, therefore, a moment or if, after reflection, you produce an intricate or profound argument, you,
in a manner, give up the question and confess that it is not
reasoning which engages us to suppose the past resembling the
future, and to expect similar effects from causes which are
to appearance similar. This is the proposition which I intended to enforce in the present section. If I be right, I
pretend not to have made any mighty discovery. And if I be
wrong, I must acknowledge myself to be indeed a very backward
scholar, since I cannot now discover an argument which, it
seems, was perfectly familiar to me long before I was out of
my cradle.

JOHN STUART MILL

THE GROUND OF INDUCTION

AXIOM OF THE UNIFORMITY OF THE COURSE OF NATURE

Induction properly so called, as distinguished from those
mental operations, sometimes, though improperly designated by
the name, which I have attempted /earlier/ to characterize,
may, then, be summarily defined as generalization from experience. It consists in inferring from some individual instances
in which a phenomenon is observed to occur that it occurs in
all instances of a certain class, namely, in all which *resemble*
the former in what are regarded as the material circumstances.

In what way the material circumstances are to be distinguished from those which are immaterial, or why some of the
circumstances are material and others not so, we are not yet
ready to point out. We must first observe that there is a
principle implied in the very statement of what induction is;
an assumption with regard to the course of nature and the order
of the universe, namely, that there are such things in nature
as parallel cases; that what happens once will, under a sufficient degree of similarity of circumstances, happen again,
and not only again, but as often as the same circumstances
recur. This, I say, is an assumption involved in every case
of induction. And, if we consult the actual course of nature,
we find that the assumption is warranted. The universe, so
far as known to us, is so constituted that whatever is true
in any one case is true in all cases of a certain description;
the only difficulty is to find what description.

This universal fact, which is our warrant for all inferences from experience, has been described by different

From John Stuart Mill, A *System of Logic,* 10th ed., Book
III, Chaps. 3 and 21, Longmans, Green & Co., London, 1879.

philosophers in different forms of language: that the course
of nature is uniform; that the universe is governed by general
laws; and the like. . . .

Whatever be the most proper mode of expressing it, the
proposition that the course of nature is uniform is the fundamental principle or general axiom of induction. It would yet
be a great error to offer this large generalization as any
explanation of the inductive process. On the contrary, I hold
it to be itself an instance of induction, and induction by no
means of the most obvious kind. Far from being the first induction we make, it is one of the last or, at all events, one
of those which are latest in attaining strict philosophical
accuracy. As a general maxim, indeed, it has scarcely entered
into the minds of any but philosophers; nor even by them, as
we shall have many opportunities of remarking, have its extent
and limits been always very justly conceived. The truth is
that this great generalization is itself founded on prior generalizations. The obscurer laws of nature were discovered by
means of it, but the more obvious ones must have been understood and assented to as general truths before it was ever
heard of. We should never have thought of affirming that all
phenomena take place according to general laws if we had not
first arrived, in the case of a great multitude of phenomena,
at some knowledge of the laws themselves, which could be done
no otherwise than by induction. In what sense, then, can a
principle which is so far from being our earliest induction be
regarded as our warrant for all the others? In the only sense
in which (as we have already seen) the general propositions
which we place at the head of our reasonings when we throw
them into syllogisms ever really contribute to their validity.
As Archbishop Whately remarks, every induction is a syllogism
with the major premise suppressed; or (as I prefer expressing
it) every induction may be thrown into the form of a syllogism
by supplying a major premise. If this be actually done, the
principle which we are now considering, that of the uniformity
of the course of nature, will appear as the ultimate major
premise of all inductions and will, therefore, stand to all
inductions in the relation in which, as has been shown at so
much length, the major proposition of a syllogism always stands
to the conclusion, not contributing at all to prove, but being
a necessary condition of its being proved; since no conclusion
is proved for which there cannot be found a true major premise.

The statement that the uniformity of the course of nature is the ultimate major premise in all cases of induction may be thought to require some explanation. The immediate major premise in every inductive argument it certainly is not. Of that, Archbishop Whately's must be held to be the correct account. The induction, "John, Peter, etc., are mortal, therefore all mankind are mortal," may, as he justly says, be thrown into a syllogism by prefixing as a major premise (what is at any rate a necessary condition of the validity of the argument), namely, that what is true of John, Peter, etc., is true of all mankind. But how came we by this major premise? It is not self-evident; nay, in all cases of unwarranted generalization, it is not true. How, then, is it arrived at? Necessarily either by induction or ratiocination; and if by induction, the process, like all other inductive arguments, may be thrown into the form of a syllogism. This previous syllogism it is, therefore, necessary to construct. There is, in the long run, only one possible construction. The real proof that what is true of John, Peter, etc., is true of all mankind can only be that a different supposition would be inconsistent with the uniformity which we know to exist in the course of nature. Whether there would be this inconsistency or not may be a matter of long and delicate inquiry, but unless there would, we have no sufficient ground for the major of the inductive syllogism. It hence appears that, if we throw the whole course of any inductive argument into a series of syllogisms, we shall arrive by more or fewer steps at an ultimate syllogism which will have for its major premise the principle or axiom of the uniformity of the course of nature.

THE LAW OF CAUSALITY DOES NOT REST ON AN INSTINCT

The validity of all the inductive methods depends on the assumption that every event, or the beginning of every phenomenon, must have some cause, some antecedent, on the existence of which it is invariably and unconditionally consequent. In the method of agreement this is obvious, that method avowedly proceeding on the supposition that we have found the true cause as soon as we have negatived every other. The assertion is equally true of the method of difference. That method authorizes us to infer a general law from two instances: one, in which A exists together with a multitude of other circumstances, and B follows; another, in which, A being removed and all other circumstances remaining the same, B is prevented. What, however, does this prove? It proves that B, in the particular instance, cannot have had any other cause than A; but to conclude from this that A was the cause or that A will on other occasions be followed by B is only allowable on the assumption that B must have some cause, that among its antecedents in any single instance in which it occurs, there must be one which has the capacity of producing it at other times. This being admitted, it is seen that in the case in question that antecedent can be no other than A; but that, if it be no other than A, it must be A is not proved; by these instances at least, but taken for granted. There is no need to spend time in proving that the same thing is true of the other inductive methods. The universality of the law of causation is assumed in them all.

But is this assumption warranted? Doubtless (it may be said) *most* phenomena are connected as effects with some antecedent or cause, that is, are never produced unless some assignable fact has preceded them, but the very circumstance that complicated processes of induction are sometimes necessary shows that cases exist in which this regular order of succession is not apparent to our unaided apprehension. If, then, the processes which bring these cases within the same category with the rest require that we should assume the universality of the very law which they do not at first sight appear to exemplify, is not this a *petitio principii*? Can we prove a proposition by an argument which takes it for granted? And if not so proved, on what evidence does it rest?

For this difficulty, which I have purposely stated in the strongest terms it will admit of, the school of metaphysicians who have long predominated in this country find a ready salvo. They affirm that the universality of causation is a truth which we cannot help believing, that the belief in it is an instinct, one of the laws of our believing faculty. As the proof of this, they say, and they have nothing else to say, that everybody does believe it, and they number it among the propositions, rather numerous in their catalogue, which may be logically argued against and perhaps cannot be logically proved, but which are of higher authority than logic, and so essentially inherent in the human mind that even he who denies them in speculation shows by his habitual practice that his arguments make no impression upon himself.

Into the merits of this question, considered as one of psychology, it would be foreign to my purpose to enter here, but I must protest against adducing, as evidence of the truth of a fact in external nature, the disposition, however strong or however general, of the human mind to believe it. . . .

Were we to suppose (what it is perfectly possible to imagine) that the present order of the universe were brought to an end, and that a chaos succeeded in which there was no fixed succession of events, and the past gave no assurance of the future; if a human being were miraculously kept alive to witness this change, he surely would soon cease to believe in any uniformity, the uniformity itself no longer existing. If this be admitted, the belief in uniformity either is not an instinct, or it is an instinct conquerable, like all other instincts, by acquired knowledge.

BUT ON AN INDUCTION BY SIMPLE ENUMERATION

As was observed in a former place, the belief we entertain in the universality, throughout nature, of the law of cause and effect is itself an instance of induction, and by no means one of the earliest which any of us, or which mankind in general, can have made. We arrive at this universal law by generalization from many laws of inferior generality. We should never have had the notion of causation (in the philosophical meaning of the term) as a condition of all phenomena unless many cases of causation, or, in other words, many partial uniformities of sequence, had previously become familiar. The more obvious of the particular uniformities suggest and give evidence of the general uniformity, and the general uniformity, once established, enables us to prove the remainder of the particular uniformities of which it is made up. As, however, all rigorous processes of induction presuppose the general uniformity, our knowledge of the particular uniformities from which it was first inferred was not, of course, derived from rigorous induction, but from the loose and uncertain mode of induction *per enumerationem simplicem*, and the law of universal causation, being collected from results so obtained, cannot itself rest on any better foundation.

It would seem, therefore, that induction *per enumeratio-nem simplicem* not only is not necessarily an illicit logical process, but is in reality the only kind of induction possible, since the more elaborate process depends for its validity on a law itself obtained in that inartificial mode. Is there not, then, an inconsistency in contrasting the looseness of one method with the rigidity of another, when that other is indebted to the looser method for its own foundation?

The inconsistency, however, is only apparent. Assuredly, if induction by simple enumeration were an invalid process, no process grounded on it could be valid; just as no reliance could be placed on telescopes if we could not trust our eyes. But though a valid process, it is a fallible one, and fallible in very different degrees; if, therefore, we can substitute for the more fallible forms of the process an operation grounded on the same process in a less fallible form, we shall have effected a very material improvement. And this is what scientific induction does.

IN WHAT CASES SUCH INDUCTION IS ALLOWABLE

Now the precariousness of the method of simple enumeration is in an inverse ratio to the largeness of the generalization. The process is delusive and insufficient, exactly in proportion as the subject-matter of the observation is special and limited in extent. As the sphere widens, this unscientific method becomes less and less liable to mislead, and the most universal class of truths, the law of causation, for instance, and the principles of number and of geometry, are duly and satisfactorily proved by that method alone, nor are they susceptible of any other proof.

With respect to the whole class of generalizations of which we have recently treated, the uniformities which depend on causation, the truth of the remark just made follows by obvious inference from the principles laid down /earlier/. When a fact has been observed a certain number of times to be true and is not in any instance known to be false, if we at once affirm that fact as a universal truth or law of nature without either testing it by any of the methods of induction or deducing it from other known laws, we shall, in general, err grossly, but we are perfectly justified in affirming it as an empirical law, true within certain limits of time, place, and circumstance, provided the number of coincidences be greater than can with any probability be ascribed to chance. The reason for not extending it beyond those limits is that the fact of its holding true within them may be a consequence of collocations which cannot be concluded to exist in one place because they exist in another, or may be dependent on the accidental absence of counteracting agencies, which any variation of time or the smallest change of circumstances may possibly bring into play. If we suppose, then, the subject-matter of any generalization to be so widely diffused that there is no time, no place, and no combination of circumstances but must afford an example either of its truth or of its falsity, and if it be never found otherwise than true, its truth cannot be contingent on any collocations, unless such as exist at all times and places; nor can it be frustrated by any counteracting agencies, unless by such as never actually occur. It is, therefore, an empirical law co-extensive with all human experience; at which point the distinction between empirical laws and laws of nature vanishes, and the proposition takes its place among the most firmly established as well as largest truths accessible to science.

CHAPTER THREE

THE MEANING OF TRUTH

ON TRUTH

> *To say of what is that it is not, or of what is
> not that it is, is false; while to say of what is that
> it is, and of what is not that it is not, is true.*
> —Aristotle

Every claim to knowledge is also a claim to truth. In
saying he knows that grass is green, a person is saying it is
true that grass is green. And just as the philosopher is concerned with the nature of knowledge, he is also concerned with
the nature of truth. If a person believes or asserts that
such and such is true, what is there about what he believes
or says that makes it true? What, in short, is meant by
truth—as opposed to error, falsehood?

Two quite different questions concerning truth must be
distinguished. The first is strictly a question of meaning:
what is the meaning of the terms 'true' and 'false'? What
does it *mean* to say that "George Washington was the first
President of the United States" is true and that "New York
seceded from the union in 1860" is false? In other words,
how do the words 'true' and 'false' function in our language?

The second question asks how we can *know* in any given
instance what *is* true or what *is* false. What are the rules
or criteria for distinguishing between true beliefs and false
beliefs? This type of question merges with the difficult
problem of how genuine knowledge is to be distinguished from
mere belief, and thus requires an examination of the grounds
for knowledge.

It is very important to keep these different questions
separate, since any confusion between them will only compli-
cate the issues and create unnecessary problems. For present
purposes our primary concern will be the question of meaning,
which is a necessary preliminary to any further investigation.
We first of all have to determine what truth and falsehood
mean; only afterwards can we specify what particular beliefs
and claims *are true* or *are false*.

Considering the question of definition, we find within
the tradition three basic theories.

THE CORRESPONDENCE THEORY

This is the view that truth consists in some form of
agreement or 'correspondence' between a belief, or a judgment, and a fact in the real world. This is the commonsense
theory and, in one or another version, probably the most widely
held among philosophers. If I believe that Chicago is situated
north of Louisville, then my belief is true if, and only if,
it corresponds to the facts, i.e. the actual geographical situation. If the belief does not so correspond, then it is false.

According to the correspondence theory, truth and falsehood are to be understood as properties of beliefs or judgments. In ordinary language the word 'belief' is used sometimes to indicate the mental state of believing, sometimes to
indicate what is believed. Since it does not make sense to
call a psychological state true or false, it is clear that
when the theory asserts that beliefs are true, the reference
is strictly in the sense of *what is believed*. The same holds
with respect to judgment. The technical term in philosophy
for *what* we believe or judge or assert is 'proposition'; hence,
properly speaking, truth and falsehood are properties of propositions. We might better define a 'proposition' as that content or meaning expressed by sentences. For example, the two
sentences "It is raining" and "Il pleut" express the same
proposition; one sentence being English, one being French.
The sentence itself is not considered true or false, but rather
what the sentence expresses.

As an implication of this theory, it is to be observed
that the truth or falsehood of a proposition depends on

82

realities outside the mind. While it may be the case that minds create beliefs, the mind cannot make them true or false. What makes a belief (i.e. proposition) true is a fact, the very existence of which (except in special cases) is independent of the mind.[1] If I think that Adams was the first President of the United States, I think falsely, and no degree of conviction or mental effort or vividness in my thoughts can change the matter—because what determines the falsehood of the proposition is a set of facts intrinsically independent of the mind. And it is this type of reasoning which explains why the correspondence theory is readily adopted by most realists: truth becomes defined as fidelty to objective reality. Notice here that 'truth' is not synonymous with 'fact'; the former is a property of propositions, the latter is simply a state of affairs. There can be a world of facts with no propositions, but without propositions there is no truth.

While the correspondence theory seems only too obviously true, critics point out that it is far from self-evident. Here are three of the more common objections.

A. It remains unclear precisely what is meant by the key defining terms of the theory: what exactly is a *fact*? What is the nature of the *correspondence* which subsists between true beliefs and facts?

Is the term 'fact' to be understood as equivalent to 'reality' as it actually is, outside and independent of thought or experience? If so, there arises the unavoidable problem of how we can ever know that our judgments correspond with reality. Since we can never know an object or an event apart from our sense-data, and since sense-data do not reveal the nature of reality as it is in itself, it is foolish to talk about whether or not our judgments correspond with reality in itself, i.e. the facts. We cannot tell by inspecting a photograph whether it is a close resemblance of a person we have

---

[1]A special case would be one in which the fact itself is a function of the mind. For example, if I believe that I can count to ten, this belief (or proposition) is true only if it is a fact that I can count to ten, but that 'fact' itself involves the mental process of counting.

never seen.

If, however, facts are defined in terms of observable data or as being subject to empirical verification, then the basis of truth becomes a subjective set of sensations—which suggests that truth is neither objectively real nor independent of the mind. In whichever way the term 'fact' is defined, the correspondence theorist faces a problem.

And the notion of correspondence is even more perplexing. Is correspondence to be understood as a correlation or association of members of one set of things with each member of a second set and vice-versa, in the manner of a mathematical 1::1 correspondence? It is difficult to conceive what that would be like in the case of propositions and facts. What would constitute the various members of the two sets?

Might we define correspondence in terms of congruence, whereby when two things correspond there is perfect consonance and exact similarity in every detail? Is it meant that a true proposition copies or identically resembles the corresponding fact? This too incorporates difficulties. How can a belief or proposition—which is mental—identically resemble something which is not mental, i.e. a fact? Judgments are not *like* the physical states of affairs to which they refer. We express propositions with words, but words are not in the least similar to the facts which they indicate. Furthermore, even if it could be shown that true propositions, while not corresponding 100 percent, do have a *high degree* of correspondence with the facts, there would be an endless debate as to the actual break off point along the scale of degree determining what is true and what is false.

The correspondence theory does not give us much information—least of all does it explain the meaning of truth—unless we can succeed in defining correspondence, but as yet no one has been able to provide a satisfactory definition.

B. Since the word 'true' is an adjective which purportedly designates a certain property of propositions, it would seem that one should be able to determine whether a proposition has such property merely by scrupulously examining it. If a

a book has the property 'brown', this can be shown by looking
at the book, closely observing it. But even on common sense
it is evident that in determining whether the proposition "It
is raining outside" is true, we need to examine *something
other* than just the proposition, namely, we must go outside
and look. If truth is a property of propositions, it seems
as though it is a very peculiar kind of property.

A possible response is that truth is a relational property, indicating a special type of relation--i.e. one of cor-
respondence--between a proposition and a fact. Just as 'north
of' specifies a property of Canada *in relation* to the United
States, so also 'true' refers to a property of a proposition
in relation to a state of affairs.

However, to call truth a relational property merely com-
pounds the problem. Any meaningful relation presupposes at
least two elements. The phrase "Canada is north of _____"
just does not make sense unless we fill in the blank. Yet
there are many examples of supposedly true propositions in
which it is not clear whether there is anything relationally
corresponding. Consider true propositions about the future.
What *is there* to which these propositions correspond, since
the future does not yet exist? What about hypothetical propositions, such as "If the basketball team would have lost the
game, the cheerleaders would have cried"? This might be a
true proposition, but supposing that the team in fact won the
game there seems to be no *fact* in the existent world to which
this proposition is related. How then can it be claimed that
truth is a relational property of the proposition--when there
is no existent *fact* to which the proposition is related?

Whether it is claimed that truth is a property or that
it is a relation, there are crucial problems of clarification
that need to be reckoned with to adequately defend the correspondence theory.

C. Perhaps the most interesting objection is that any
attempt to prove the truth of the correspondence theory by
way of its own methodology necessarily leads to an infinite
regress. This can be seen as follows:

85

1. Statement of the correspondence theory in proposi-
tional form: (P_1) "The truth of a proposition consists in its
correspondence with a fact."

2. (P_1) is either true or false: if false, that explicitly means that the correspondence theory itself is false; if
true, then it is so only in virtue of corresponding with some
fact, which we can symbolize (F_1). [Hypothetical query: what
kind of fact might (F_1) be? Where do we find it? How can we
know it?]

3. Supposing that indeed (P_1) corresponds to (F_1), then
we can construct a new proposition: (P_2) "(P_1) corresponds to
(F_1)."

4. (P_2) is either true or false: if false, then by implication the correspondence theory—i.e. (P_1)—is itself
false; if true, then it is so only in virtue of corresponding
with some other fact, which we can symbolize (F_2).

5. Supposing that indeed (P_2) corresponds to (F_2), then
we can construct a new proposition: (P_3) "(P_2) corresponds to
(F_2)."

6. (P_3) is either true or false: . . .

.
.
.

Ad infinitum!

It should be noted that in itself an infinite regress
does not constitute a direct refutation of that which ini-
tiates it. However, the fact that a philosophical theory
harbors within itself an infinite regress often is interpreted
as an objectionable weakness and a mark of inadequacy. In
any case, as formulated above the predicament seems inescapable.

THE COHERENCE THEORY

This theory, generally associated with idealists, maintains that truth is not constituted by a relationship between a proposition and something else, a fact or reality, but by a relationship of harmony or consistency among a set of propositions. This formulation avoids the major difficulties surrounding the correspondence theory, since there is no need for direct access to some underlying reality. A given proposition is said to be true if it is consistent with other propositions already regarded as true. True beliefs are those which logically cohere with other relevant beliefs. Truth, therefore, is defined as a function of propositions 'fitting together' within a generally accepted framework.

A working model for the coherence theory is Euclidean geometry. Building upon a number of axioms and postulates accepted as being true, an entire system of 'truths' can be constructed, where the truth of each theorem is a function of its logical consistency with the rest of the system. The principle of consistency, based on the law of noncontradiction—that something cannot both *be* and *not be* at the same time—underlies any science or organized body of knowledge. Even in everyday life we often judge a statement to be true or false on the grounds of its coherence with what we have already decided is true. It is on this basis that we renounce many ideas as absurd and label certain experiences as illusions or hallucinations—they just do not fit into the accepted system of thought.

Historically there have been two basic criticisms of the coherence theory.

A. Consistency is a mark of internal relatedness among a set of beliefs or propositions. But it would seem that we can construct false as well as true coherent systems. So a new proposition can indeed fit coherently with a large number of previously accepted propositions; but what if these latter all happen actually to be false! The coherence theory simply is incapable of discriminating between consistent truth and consistent error. What if a new proposition fits into one system but is in disharmony with a different system: is it to be considered *both* true and false; or is one body of beliefs to be given priority over the other—but if so, upon what criteria?

As examples critics point to past systems of belief which, though internally consistent, ultimately have been rejected as false. The Ptolemic theory that the earth was the center of the solar system, as a result of its coherence, held sway for 1500 years, but was at last displaced in favor of the Copernican theory—an opposite yet itself internally consistent world view. Other obvious examples include the widespread acceptance of the biological theory of evolution, also the reception of Einstein's theory of relativity.

B. The attempt to define truth in terms of logical coherence ultimately leads to a vicious circle. The very notion of coherence, the critics argue, already presupposes truth. To say that A coheres with B is to assert that A is logically consistent with B; but this is to assert precisely that A and B can both be true at the same time, that they are not logically contradictory. But to know that A and B can both be true at the same time presupposes that we know what truth is, namely, what it means for A to be true and B to be true. Supposedly the very purpose of the coherence theory is to define the meaning of truth, but now it seems that coherence is itself defined in terms of truth—hence the circularity.

THE PRAGMATIC THEORY

Pragmatism is an essentially American philosophy which gained notoriety during the early 1900's, primarily through the writings of Charles S. Peirce (1839-1914), William James (1842-1910), and John Dewey (1859-1942). The pragmatic theory of truth is but one of many features within pragmatism as a whole. It also should be noted that there are differing versions of the pragmatic theory, depending on which particular author we turn to, though it was James who wrote the most regarding the meaning of truth.

Generally speaking, pragmatism defines truth in terms of usefulness or workability. The truth-value of a belief or proposition is determined directly by its results: if an idea works out in practice, if accepting it leads to satisfactory consequences, then it is true. In short, the pragmatic view can be stated thusly: if something works, it is true!

The phrase 'satisfactory consequences' requires further elucidation. *Satisfactory* in what respect?--Psychological contentment? Fulfillment of human desires? Gratification of individual whims? Satisfactory *for whom?*--One individual? Many individuals? All men? Satisfactory *for how long?*-- Today? Tomorrow also? Forever? There would seem to be de-grees of satisfaction, contentment, fulfillment, gratification; does this mean likewise that there are degrees of truth? These and other questions need to be answered before there can be any adequate evaluation of the pragmatic theory.

To begin with, 'satisfaction' is not to be understood merely as a psychological or emotional attitude, but more ac-curately as the embodiment or concrete expression of empirical verification. True ideas are those which can be demonstrated experimentally. The pragmatic view here reflects the practice of modern science. When a question of truth or falsity arises, be it in the laboratory or in daily life, the pragmatic method is to *experiment and see.* In the words of William James, *"True ideas are those that we can assimilate, validate, corroborate, and verify. False ideas are those that we cannot."*[1] And John Dewey echoes this same principle: "The hypothesis that works is the true one; and *truth* is an abstract noun applied to the collection of cases, actual, foreseen and desired, that receive confirmation in their works and consequences."[2]

Empirical verification is never absolute, since the test-ing process theoretically has no limit; therefore neither is truth absolute. For the pragmatist, there is no such thing as static or absolute truth--truth.is subject to change!   To

---

[1]William James, "Pragmatism's Conception of Truth," in *The Writings of William James* , ed. by John J. McDermott (New York: Random House, Inc., 1967), p. 430.

[2]John Dewey, *Reconstruction in Philosophy* (New York: Henry Holt and Company, 1920), pp. 156-57.

illustrate this, at one time it was believed that the earth was the center of the solar system, and this belief had the scientific confirmation of the day; the pragmatist would maintain that at that point in time the belief *was true*, it worked, it satisfactorily explained certain phenomena, it had empirical validation. As time progressed, however, the belief became less and less satisfactory, it left unexplained more and more types of observations, until finally it became rejected and replaced with a 'more workable' theory, à la Copernicus. In short, just as the belief had at first *become* true, it later *became* false. As James declares, truth is something that *happens* to an idea, in a sense *truths are created.* The relativity of truth is demonstrated by the fact that a judgment is true as long as it works yet becomes false when it ceases to have practical utility.

To some extent pragmatists are subjectivists. Indeed, truth is conceived as being subjective, though not in the sense of idealism. Rather, the subjectivity of all truth is the result of its being grounded in human experience and tied to human practice. The proposition "Bread is a source of nourishment" can be deemed true on the basis of nutritional research and scientific experimentation, as well as on grounds of everyday practice. The *truth* of the proposition is not some 'objectivity' waiting to be discovered, but is a product of human subjectivity by way of experience, observation, verification, and practice.

The final point of clarification which needs to be made is that subjectivity, for the pragmatists, does not imply privacy. To say that truth is subjective is not to say that truth is a matter of individual whim or personal preference. The notion of workability must not be reduced to the satisfying of personal desires. It is surely the case that some types of beliefs can be verified privately and purely to one's own satisfaction. For example, if I happen to find a certain statement funny, then it is true (for me) that the statement *is* funny—though no one else might think so. However, any belief that pertains to more than one person requires public confirmation. A person might fervently believe that sugar is a cure for cancer, and perhaps this belief proved satisfactory when he developed stomach cancer, consumed large quantities of sugar over a period of time, and was 'miraculously' cured; still, this type of 'satisfaction' does not by itself constitute sufficient verification of the belief's truth. Why? Because the belief is about something public—the cure for cancer—which therefore requires public verification. In other words, unless the cure is similarly evidenced in other cancer patients, the pragmatist will firmly claim, presently at least, that the belief is false.

The following types of objections have been raised against the pragmatic theory.

A. While beliefs that are true tend to work in the long run, it is not necessarily the case that beliefs which work are therefore true. Innumerable theories—in religion, science, medicine, and other fields—have 'worked' for long periods of time, yet in the end have been proven false.

B. Furthermore, the notion that truth is subject to change over periods of time is repugnant to our commonsense intuitions. That the earth is the center of the solar system either *is true* or *is false*—and that's that! Its truth or falsity is not a matter of belief, not a matter of workability, but strictly a matter of reality. While it may be the case that our beliefs about this reality may change, and while the practical utility of our beliefs may rise or fall, truth itself remains constant. Any theory which claims otherwise is simply mistaken.

C. If a proposition is true at all, it surely must be true for everybody. If it is true that George Washington was the first President of the United States, then it will always be true, and will not become false in some future generation should the results of believing it happen to prove dissatisfying. Just because an idea works for one person and may not work for another, it does not follow that the idea is true for the one and false for the other. A single proposition cannot at the same time be both true and false. Some people believe that man is free, while others believe that man is totally determined by outside factors: obviously both views cannot be true—no matter how well each may 'work' for the respective believers!

SUMMARY

We began with the question as to the meaning of truth.
Three traditional theories have been discussed, each exhibit-
ing certain strengths as well as shortcomings. It may be
that no one theory is complete in itself, and that the meaning of truth can be fully defined only by some combination of
the different views. Perhaps there are two kinds of truth--
subjective and objective, truth as individually experienced
and truth as it actually is. Perhaps an entirely different
sort of theory is required to sufficiently define truth; somewhat recent attempts include the redundancy theory,[1] the semantic theory,[2] and the performative theory.[3]

Then again, it may be that ultimately truth is incapable
of being defined in terms other than of itself, in this respect
analogous, for example, to the color yellow. It has sometimes
been argued that just as it is impossible to describe yellow
to someone who has always been blind, it is equally impossible
to explain the meaning of truth to someone who does not already
understand it. However, even if truth is indefinable, philosophers may still inquire about its relations, its criteria,
and in particular how specific truths or falsehoods can be
actually known.

---

[1] See F. P. Ramsey, "Facts and Propositions," *Proceedings of the Aristotelian Society*, supp. vol. VII (1927).

[2] Alfred Tarski, "The Semantic Conception of Truth and the Foundations of Semantics," *Philosophy and Phenomenological Research*, vol. IV (1944).

[3] P. F. Strawson, "Truth," *Analysis*, vol. IX (1949).

BERTRAND RUSSELL

A CORRESPONDENCE THEORY OF TRUTH

A. FACT

"Fact," as I intend the term, can only be defined ostensively. Everything that there is in the world I call a "fact."
The sun is a fact; Caesar's crossing of the Rubicon was a fact;
if I have a toothache, my toothache is a fact. If I make a
statement, my making it is a fact, and if it is true there is
a further fact in virtue of which it is true, but not if it is
false. The butcher says, "I'm sold out, and that's a fact";
immediately afterward, a favored customer arrives and gets a
nice piece of lamb from under the counter. So the butcher
told two lies, one in saying he was sold out and the other in
saying that his being sold out was a fact. Facts are what make
statements true or false. I should like to confine the word
"fact" to the minimum of what must be known in order that the
truth or falsehood of any statement may follow analytically
from those asserting that minimum. For example, if "Brutus
was a Roman" and "Cassius was a Roman" each assert a fact, I
should not say that "Brutus and Cassius were Romans" asserted
a new fact. . . .

I mean by a "fact" something which is there, whether anybody thinks so or not. If I look up a railway timetable and
find that there is a train to Edinburgh at 10 A.M., then, if
the timetable is correct, there is an actual train, which is
a "fact." The statement in the timetable is itself a "fact,"
whether true or false, but it only *states* a fact if it is true,

From Bertrand Russell, *Human Knowledge: Its Scope and
Limits,* c 1948 by Bertrand Russell, renewed (c) 1975 by the
estate of Bertrand Russell. Reprinted by permission of SIMON
& SCHUSTER, a Division of Gulf & Western Corporation.

i.e., if there really is a train. Most facts are independent of our volitions; that is why they are called "hard," "stubborn," or "ineluctable." Physical facts, for the most part, are independent, not only of our volitions but even of our existence.

The whole of our cognitive life is, biologically considered, part of the process of adaptation to facts. This process is one which exists, in a greater or less degree, in all forms of life, but is not commonly called "cognitive" until it reaches a certain level of development. Since there is no sharp frontier anywhere between the lowest animal and the most profound philosopher, it is evident that we cannot say precisely at what point we pass from mere animal behavior to something deserving to be dignified by the name of "knowledge." But at every stage there is adaptation, and that to which the animal adapts itself is the environment of *fact.*

B. BELIEF

"Belief," which we have next to consider, has an inherent and inevitable vagueness, which is due to the continuity of mental development from the amoeba to *homo sapiens.* In its most developed form, which is that most considered by philosophers, it is displayed by the assertion of a sentence. After sniffing for a time, you exclaim, "Good heavens! The house is on fire." Or, when a picnic is in contemplation, you say, "Look at those clouds. There will be rain." Or, in a train, you try to subdue an optimistic fellow-passenger by observing, "Last time I did this journey we were three hours late." Such remarks, if you are not lying, express beliefs. We are so accustomed to the use of words for expressing beliefs that it may seem strange to speak of "belief" in cases where there are no words. But it is clear that even when words are used they are not of the essence of the matter. The smell of burning first makes you believe that the house is on fire, and then the words come, not as *being* the belief but as a way of putting it into a form of behavior in which it can be communicated to others. I am thinking, of course, of beliefs that are not very complicated or refined. I believe that the angles of a polygon add up to twice as many right angles as the figure has sides diminished by four right angles, but a man would

94

need superhuman mathematical intuition to be able to believe this without words. But the simpler kind of belief, especially when it calls for action, may be entirely unverbalized. When you are traveling with a companion, you may say, "We must run; the train is just going to start." But if you are alone you may have the same belief, and run just as fast, without any words passing through your head.

I propose, therefore, to treat belief as something that can be pre-intellectual, and can be displayed in the behavior of animals. I incline to think that, on occasion, a purely bodily state may deserve to be called a "belief." For example, if you walk into your room in the dark and someone has put a chair in an unusual place, you may bump into it, because your body believed there was no chair there. But the parts played by mind and body respectively in belief are not very important to separate for our present purposes. A belief, as I understand the term, is a certain kind of state of body or mind or both. To avoid verbiage, I shall call it a state of an organism, and ignore the distinction of bodily and mental factors.

One characteristic of a belief is that it has external reference, . . . The simplest case, which can be observed behavioristically, is when, owing to a conditioned reflex, the presence of A causes behavior appropriate to B. This covers the important case of acting on information received: here the phrase heard is A, and what it signifies is B. Somebody says, "Look out, there's a car coming," and you act as you would if you saw the car. In this case you are believing what is signified by the phrase "a car is coming."

Any state of an organism which consists in believing something can, theoretically, be fully described without mentioning the something. When you believe "a car is coming," your belief consists in a certain state of the muscles, sense-organs, and emotions, together perhaps with certain visual images. All this, and whatever else may go to make up your belief, could, in theory, be fully described by a psychologist and physiologist working together, without their ever having to mention anything outside your mind and body. Your state, when you believe that a car is coming, will be very different in different circumstances. You may be watching a race, and wondering

whether the car on which you have put your money will win.
You may be waiting for the return of your son from captivity
in the Far East. You may be trying to escape from the police.
You may be suddenly roused from absent-mindedness while crossing the street. But although your total state will not be
the same in these various cases, there will be something in
common among them, and it is this something which makes them
all instances of the belief that a car is coming. A belief,
we may say, is a collection of states of an organism bound
together by all having in whole or part the same external reference.

     In an animal or a young child, believing is shown by an
action or series of actions. The beliefs of the hound about
the fox are shown by his following the scent. But in human
beings, as a result of language and of the practice of suspended reactions, believing often becomes a more or less static
condition, consisting perhaps in pronouncing or imagining appropriate words, together with one of the feelings that constitute different kinds of belief. As to these, we may enumerate: first, the kind of belief that consists in filling out
sensations by animal inferences; second, memory; third, expectation; fourth, the kind of belief resulting from conscious
inference; and fifth, the kind of belief generated unreflect-
ingly by testimony. Perhaps this list is both incomplete and
in part redundant, but certainly perception, memory, and expectation differ as to the kinds of feeling involved. "Belief,"
therefore, is a wide generic term, and a state of believing is
not sharply separated from cognate states which would not naturally be described as believings.

     The question what it is that is believed when an organism
is in a state of believing is usually somewhat vague. The
hound pursuing a scent is unusually definite, because his purpose is simple and he has no doubt as to the means; but a
pigeon hesitating whether to eat out of your hand is in a
much more vague and complex condition. Where human beings
are concerned, language gives an illusory appearance of precision; a man may be able to express his belief in a sentence,
and it is then supposed that the sentence is what he believes.
But as a rule this is not the case. If you say, "Look, there
is Jones," you are believing something, and expressing your

belief in words, but what you are believing has to do with
Jones, not with the name "Jones." You may, on another occasion, have a belief which *is* concerned with words: "Who is
that very distinguished man who has just come in? That is
Sir Theophilus Thwackum." In this case it is the name you
want. But as a rule in ordinary speech the words are, so to
speak, transparent; they are not what is believed, any more
than a man is the name by which he is called.

When words merely *express* a belief which is about what
the words mean, the belief indicated by the words is lacking
in precision to the degree that the meaning of the words is
lacking in precision. Outside logic and pure mathematics,
there are no words of which the meaning is precise, not even
such words as "centimeter" and "second." Therefore even when
a belief is expressed in words having the greatest degree of
precision of which empirical words are capable, the question
as to what it is that is believed is still more or less vague.

This vagueness does not cease when a belief is what may
be called "purely verbal," i.e., when what is believed is that
a certain sentence is true. This is the sort of belief acquired by schoolboys whose education has been on old-fashioned
lines. Consider the difference in the schoolboy's attitude
to "William the Conqueror, 1066" and "Next Wednesday will be
a whole holiday." In the former case, he knows that that is
the right form of words, and cares not a pin for their meaning; in the latter case, he acquires a belief about next Wednesday, and cares not a pin what words you use to generate
his belief. The former belief, but not the latter is "purely
verbal."

If I were to say that the schoolboy is believing that the
sentence "William the Conqueror, 1066" is "true," I should
have to add that his definition of "truth" is purely pragmatic:
a sentence is "true" if the consequences of uttering it in the
presence of a master are pleasant; if they are unpleasant, it
is "false."

Forgetting the schoolboy, and resuming our proper character as philosophers, what do *we* mean when we say that a
certain sentence is "true"? I am not yet asking what is meant
by "true"; this will be our next topic. For the moment I am

concerned to point out that however "true" may be defined, the significance of "This sentence is true" must depend upon the significance of the sentence, and is therefore vague in exactly the degree in which there is vagueness in the sentence which is said to be true. We do not therefore escape from vagueness by concentrating attention on purely verbal beliefs.

Philosophy, like science, should realize that, while complete precision is impossible, techniques can be invented which gradually diminish the area of vagueness or uncertainty. However admirable our measuring apparatus may be, there will always remain some lengths concerning which we are in doubt whether they are greater than, less than, or equal to a meter; but there is no known limit to the refinements by which the number of such doubtful lengths can be diminished. Similarly, when a belief is expressed in words, there will always remain a band of possible circumstances concerning which we cannot say whether they would make the belief true or false, but the breadth of this band can be indefinitely diminished, partly by improved verbal analysis, partly by a more delicate technique in observation. Whether complete precision is or is not theoretically possible depends upon whether the physical world is discrete or continuous.

Let us now consider the case of a belief expressed in words all of which have the greatest attainable degree of precision. Suppose, for the sake of concreteness, that I believe the sentence "My height is greater than 5 ft., 8 ins., and less than 5 ft., 9 ins." Let us call this sentence "S." I am not yet asking what would make this sentence true, or what would entitle me to say that I know it; I am asking only: "What is happening in me when I have the belief which I express by the sentence S?" There is obviously no one correct answer to this question. All that can be said definitely is that I am in a state such as, if certain further things happen, will give me a feeling which might be expressed by the words "quite so," and that, now, while these things have not yet happened, I have the idea of their happening combined with the feeling expressed by the word "yes." I may, for instance, imagine myself standing against a wall on which there is a scale of feet and inches, and in imagination see the top of me head between two marks on this scale, and toward this image I may have the feeling of assent. We may take this as the essence of what may be called "static" belief, as opposed to belief shown by action: static belief consists in an idea or image combined with a yes-feeling.

C. TRUTH

I come now to the definition of "truth" and "falsehood." Certain things are evident. Truth is a property of beliefs, and derivatively of sentences which express beliefs. Truth consists in a certain relation between a belief and one or more facts other than the belief. When this relation is absent, the belief is false. A sentence may be called "true" or "false" even if no one believes it, provided that if it were believed, the belief would be true or false as the case may be.

So much, I say, is evident. But what is not evident is the nature of the relation between belief and fact that is involved, or the definition of the possible fact that will make a given belief true, or the meaning of "possible" in this phrase. Until these questions are answered we have no adequate definition of "truth."

Let us begin with the biologically earliest form of belief, which is to be seen among animals as among men. The compresence of two kinds of circumstance, A and B, if it has been frequent or emotionally interesting, is apt to have the result that when A is sensibly present, the animal reacts as it formerly reacted to B, or at any rate displays some part of this reaction. In some animals this connection may be sometimes innate, and not the result of experience. But however the connection may be brought about, when the sensible presence of A causes acts appropriate to B, we may say that the animal "believes" B to be in the environment, and that the belief is "true" if B is in the environment. If you wake a man up in the middle of the night and shout, "Fire!," he will leap from his bed even if he does not yet see or smell fire. His action is evidence of a belief which is "true" if there is fire, and "false" otherwise. Whether his belief is true depends upon a fact which may remain outside his experience. He may escape so fast that he never acquires sensible

evidence of the fire; he may fear that he will be suspected
of incendiarism and fly the country, without ever inquiring
whether there was a fire or not; nevertheless his belief remains true if there was the fact (namely fire) which constituted its external reference or significance, and if there
was not such a fact his belief remained false even if all his
friends assured him that there had been a fire.

The difference between a true and false belief is like
that between a wife and a spinster: in the case of a true
belief there is a fact to which it has a certain relation,
but in the case of a false belief there is no such fact. To
complete our definition of "truth" and "falsehood" we need
a description of the fact which would make a given belief
true, this description being one which applies to nothing if
the belief is false. Given a woman of whom we do not know
whether she is married or not, we can frame a description
which will apply to her husband if she has one, and to nothing
if she is a spinster. Such a description would be: "the man
who stood beside her in a church or registry office while
certain words were pronounced." In like manner we want a
description of the fact or facts which, if they exist, make
a belief true. Such fact or facts I call the "verifier" of
the belief.

WILLIAM JAMES

A PRAGMATIC THEORY OF TRUTH

Truth, as any dictionary will tell you, is a property of
certain of our ideas. It means their 'agreement', as falsity
means their disagreement, with 'reality'. Pragmatists and
intellectualists both accept this definition as a matter of
course. They begin to quarrel only after the question is
raised as to what may precisely be meant by the term 'agreement' and what by the term 'reality', when reality is taken
as something for our ideas to agree with.

. . . But the great assumption of the intellectualists is
that truth means essentially an inert static relation. When
you've got your true idea of anything, there's an end of the
matter. You're in possession; you *know*; you have fulfilled
your thinking destiny. You are where you ought to be mentally;
you have obeyed your categorical imperative; and nothing need
follow on that climax of your rational destiny. Epistemolog-
ically you are in stable equilibrium.

Pragmatism, on the other hand, asks its usual question.
"Grant an idea or belief to be true," it says, "what concrete
difference will its being true make in any one's actual life?"
How will the truth be realized? What experiences will be different from those which would obtain if the belief were false?
What, in short, is the truth's cash-value in experiential
terms?

The moment pragmatism asks this question, it sees the
answer: *True ideas are those that we can assimilate, validate,
corroborate and verify. False ideas are those that we can not.*

From William James, *Pragmatism*, first published in 1907.

101

That is the practical difference it makes to us to have true
ideas; that, therefore, is the meaning of truth, for it is all
that truth is known-as.

This thesis is what I have to defend. The truth of an
idea is not a stagnant property inherent in it. Truth *happens*
to an idea. It *becomes* true, is *made* true by events. Its
verity *is* in fact an event, a process: the process namely of
its verifying itself, its veri-*fication*. Its validity is the
process of its valid-*ation*.

But what do the words verification and validation themselves pragmatically mean? They again signify certain practical consequences of the verified and validated idea. It is
hard to find any one phrase that characterizes these consequences better than the ordinary agreement-formula--just such
consequences being what we have in mind whenever we say that
our ideas 'agree' with reality. They lead us, namely, through
the acts and other ideas which they instigate, into or up to,
or towards, other parts of experience with which we feel all
the while--such feeling being among our potentialities--that
the original ideas remain in agreement. The connexions and
transitions come to us from point to point as being progres-
sive, harmonious, satisfactory. This function of agreeable
leading is what we mean by an idea's verification. Such an
account is vague and it sounds at first quite trivial, but it
has results which it will take the rest of my hour to explain.

. . . You can say of it then either that 'it is useful
because it is true' or that 'it is true because it is useful'.
Both these phrases mean exactly the same thing, namely that
here is an idea that gets fulfilled and can be verified. True
is the name for whatever idea starts the verification-process,
useful is the name for its completed function in experience.
True ideas would never have been singled out as such, would
never have acquired a class-name, least of all a name suggest-
ing value, unless they had been useful from the outset in this
way. . . .

Take, for instance, yonder object on the wall. You and
I consider it to be a 'clock', although no one of us has seen
the hidden works that make it one. We let our notion pass

102

for true without attempting to verify. If truths mean verification-process essentially, ought we then to call such un-
verified truths as this abortive? No, for they form the over-
whelmingly large number of the truths we live by. Indirect
as well as direct verifications pass muster. Where circum-
stantial evidence is sufficient, we can go without eye-wit-
nessing. Just as we here assume Japan to exist without ever
having been there, because it *works* to do so, everything we
know conspiring with the belief, and nothing interfering, so
we assume that thing to be a clock. We *use* it as a clock,
regulating the length of our lecture by it. The verification
of the assumption here means its leading to no frustration or
contradiction. Verifi*ability* of wheels and weights and pen-
dulum is as good as verification. For one truth-process completed there are a million in our lives that function in this
state of nascency. They turn us *towards* direct verification;
lead us into the *surroundings* of the objects they envisage;
and then, if everything runs on harmoniously, we are so sure
that verification is possible that we omit it, and are usually
justified by all that happens.

    Truth lives, in fact, for the most part on a credit sys-
tem. Our thoughts and beliefs 'pass', so long as nothing
challenges them, just as bank-notes pass so long as nobody
refuses them. But this all points to direct face-to-face
verifications somewhere, without which the fabric of truth
collapses like a financial system with no cash-basis whatever.
You accept my verification of one thing, I yours of another.
We trade on each other's truth. But beliefs verified concretely
by *somebody* are the posts of the whole superstructure.

                    • • •

    *Indirectly or only potentially verifying processes may
thus be true as well as full verification-processes.* They
work as true processes would work, give us the same advantages,
and claim our recognition for the same reasons. All this on
the common-sense level of matters of fact, which we are alone
considering.

                    • • •

Our account of truth is an account of truths in the plural, of processes of leading, realized *in rebus*, and having only this quality in common, that they *pay*. They pay by guiding us into or towards some part of a system that dips at numerous points into sense-percepts, which we may copy mentally or not, but with which at any rate we are now in the kind of commerce vaguely designated as verification. Truth for us is simply a collective name for verification-processes, just as health, wealth, strength, etc., are names for other processes connected with life, and also pursued because it pays to pursue them. Truth is *made*, just as health, wealth, and strength are made, in the course of experience.

. . .

'The true', to put it very briefly, is only the expedient in the way of our thinking, just as 'the right' is only the expedient in the way of our behaving. Expedient in almost any fashion; and expedient in the long run and on the whole of course; for what meets expediently all the experience in sight won't necessarily meet all farther experiences equally satisfactorily. Experience, as we know, has ways of *boiling over*, and making us correct our present formulas.

The 'absolutely' true, meaning what no farther experience will ever alter, is that ideal vanishing-point towards which we imagine that all our temporary truths will some day converge. It runs on all fours with the perfectly wise man, and with the absolutely complete experience; and, if these ideals are ever realized, they will all be realized together. Meanwhile we have to live to-day by what truth we can get to-day, and be ready to-morrow to call it falsehood. Ptolemaic astronomy, euclidean space, aristotelian logic, scholastic metaphysics, were expedient for centuries, but human experience has boiled over those limits, and we now call these things only relatively true, or true within those borders of experience. 'Absolutely' they are false; for we know that those limits were casual, and might have been transcended by past theorists just as they are by present thinkers.

104

CHAPTER FOUR

FACTS AND VALUES

ETHICAL INQUIRY

THE NATURE OF VALUES

Value judgments are those that assess the worth of objects, acts, attitudes, even people. For example, "This is a good apple," "A son should not lie to his father," and "Abortion is wrong" are value judgments. While the first example is a judgment of nonmoral value, the latter two can be classified as judgments of moral value, essentially relating to prescribed standards for human conduct.

Our everyday lives are determined to a high degree by what we value. What type of job we have, who we associate with, what organizations we belong to, who we voted for at the last presidential election, what hobbies we have, how we spend our money . . . are all a reflection of our personal values. Indeed, our values shape our thoughts, feelings, and actions, and they guide our choices and give direction to our lives. Because we believe that some ends are more worthwhile than others, our individual values determine the ultimate goals we seek in life.

But what about these values that play such an important role in people's lives? We have roughly defined value as an assessment of worth. But assessment on what basis? What standards are to be employed? What critieria are to be used? What reasons, what justification can be given in defense of particular value judgments? What happens when a person's values conflict with one another, or when one person's values conflict with those of another person? How are value judgments like judgments of fact? How are they different? Are value judgments subject to truth and error? If so, what are the criteria for determining whether a value judgment is true or

false? These are just some of the questions that arise once
we begin to study the nature of human values.

Within this context the primary philosophical concern is
in particular the nature of moral value. What constitutes
good and bad, right and wrong, just and unjust? What are the
normative principles for morally proper conduct? The study
of moral values is called *ethics*.

INTRODUCTION TO ETHICS

While in ordinary speech the words 'morals' and 'ethics'
are employed interchangeably, philosophers often discriminate
between the two terms. By morals (or morality) is meant the
normative human conduct itself, whereas ethics (or ethical)
refers specifically to the study of moral conduct and moral
values.

There are three major brances of ethics:

(1) *Descriptive ethics* is the empirical investigation of
moral phenomena as manifest in concrete socio-historical situations. The goal is to accurately describe the prevailing morality of a given people, society, or culture. The method is
strictly scientific, involving the observation of people's
actions in different situations, the collection of data about
human behavior, and the drawing of conclusions based upon the
evidence. Descriptive ethics is the concern of social psychol-
ogists, anthropologists, and historians. The aim of the philosopher, on the other hand, is not simply to describe the
morals of a people, but to inquire regarding the truth and
justification of certain moral systems.

(2) *Normative or prescriptive ethics* is concerned less
with describing how people do in fact behave, and more with
prescribing how they *ought to* behave. The primary aim is to
demonstrate a rational ground for moral obligation, and to do
so by establishing a system of moral norms or prescriptive
principles of action which can be proven valid for all mankind. By ascertaining workable rules of conduct, and by justifying certain underlying principles or standards of moral
evaluation, the philosopher seeks to develop a sound foundation

for morality, with the result that men may choose their own actions with greater understanding and be able to more adequately evaluate the practices of others.

Numerous normative ethical theories have been advanced which purport to tell us how we should conduct our lives and how in given situations we can correctly decide what is right or wrong, good or bad. Some of the more traditional theories will be described briefly later on.

(3) *Meta-ethics*, sometimes called critical or analytical ethics, concentrates on language, reasoning, and logical structures, rather than on conduct. The task here is to clarify the terminology used in ethical discourse and to elucidate the kinds of reasoning employed in justifying ethical statements. The operating methodology is that of conceptual analysis. Whereas normative ethics attempts to answer questions regarding what is right, what is good, and what is dutiful, meta-ethics responds to the more immediate problem: what do the words 'right', 'good', and 'duty' *mean* ? This is a question of language. In a sense, meta-ethics must be considered as logically prior to normative ethics, since the meta-ethical questions must be answered before the complete development of any normative system is even possible.

The bulk of contemporary moral philosophy falls into the category of meta-ethics. The selection from Moore and the essay on 'emotivism' which follow later in this chapter are examples of meta-ethical inquiry. The results of this type of analysis can provide us with a more refined understanding of moral concepts and a greater awareness of how such notions as virtue, duty, and responsibility meaningfully function in moral thinking.

SOME NORMATIVE ETHICAL THEORIES

Within the philosophical tradition two types of normative ethical theories can be distinguished: consequentialist and nonconsequentialist. According to consequentialist (or teleological) theories the morality of an action is determined by its overall consequences. Egoism and utilitarianism are teleological theories. Nonconsequentialist (or deontological) theories, on the other hand, maintain that the rightness or wrongness of an action is based on something other than the consequences. The most obvious example of a deontological theory is the Divine Command Theory, according to which an action is right and people are good if and only if they follow God's commandments, regardless of the consequences that might result.

Ethical egoism is the view that we should always act in a way that promotes our own best long-term interests. This is not to be equated with selfishness, since acting selfishly might not be in an individual's best interest—he might become disliked and lose his friends, maybe his job. The morally praiseworthy person is the one who actively pursues his own individual happiness. When faced with a moral decision, the egoist tells us to consider the consequences of the various alternatives, then choose that action which will bring about the greatest personal happiness.

In evaluating ethical egoism, important questions to be considered include: what constitutes one's best interest? What constitutes happiness? How can we ever know the long-term consequences of any act? If we cannot, then how can we ever know which actions are right? What happens when two or more people's interests conflict? How can moral arguments be resolved?

Utilitarianism, which derives its name from 'utility', meaning usefulness, is the theory that an act is right if it is useful in bringing about a desirable end. In contrast to egoism, this theory claims that in making ethical judgments we must evaluate the consequences of an action in the light of how much good will acrue for *everyone*, not just ourselves. The substance of the theory is that everyone should act so as to bring about the greatest good (or happiness) for the greatest number. John Stuart Mill is the most famous advocate of utilitarianism.

Utilitarianism is generally found in two main forms: *act utilitarianism* and *rule utilitarianism*. Act utilitarianism essentially states that we should act in such a way that our action produces the greatest happiness for the most people.

110

We cannot rely on any so-called rules for action, since each act and each situation is different. In morally evaluating any act, the total consequences for all people concerned must be determined; if the consequences are good, so is the action. For the act utilitarian, the end justifies the means.

Rule utilitarianism maintains that we should act in such a way that the rule governing our action produces the greatest happiness for the greatest number. The idea is to set up a series of rules which, when followed, will yield the greatest good for all humanity. Such rules might include "never kill except in self-defense," "obey the laws of a democratic society," and "honor the terms of freely-entered contracts." If following a given rule yields the greatest utility-value for all concerned, then the right thing to do is follow the rule—even though in this particular set of circumstances the results may be undesirable!

Though one of the most popular normative ethical theories, utilitarianism raises some perplexing problems. As in the case of any consequentialist theory, how can we ever know *all* the consequences of a given act? In particular, how can we ever determine the greatest good' for the 'greatest number'? Is goodness and happiness to be measured in terms of *quantity* or *quality*? How can one person measure the quality of goodness for someone else? Does a high quality of happiness for one person override a tiny bit of happiness for a large number of people? Furthermore, is it truly the case that the end justifies the means? Is it morally right to lie, cheat, or even murder to facilitate the goal of the greatest good for the greatest number? Against rule utilitarianism, can it reasonably be admitted that following a rule is right even if in the given situation it creates extremely horrendous consequences?

Intuitionism. Just as utilitarianism falls into two categories, act and rule, so do deontological theories. Act deontology—intuitionism—defends the position that the morality of an act is a function strictly of the particular act itself, without reference to the attending consequences. Every situation is unique and hence must be morally approached as one of a kind: generalizations, rules, and consequences are irrelevant

111

to moral evaluation. How does one decide what is the right action to take in a given situation? The act deontologist tells us it is a matter of intuition.

The problems with this view seem obvious. Is there really nothing more to rely on than our intuitions? If different people's intuitions conflict, is there no way to resolve a moral dispute? It would seem that 'justifying' a moral judgment on the basis of personal intuition is actually no justification whatsoever.

Rule deontology is the type of ethical theory which bases morality strictly upon a set of fundamental moral rules. Those acts which accord with the rule(s) are bad—irrespective of the ensuing consequences. Rule deontological theories differ precisely in respect to the particular rules which they establish.

One such theory states that the rules to be followed are the Ten Commandments laid down by God in the Old Testament. Needless to say, any justification for this theory depends on a proof for the existence of God. In addition, there would have to be some means for accurately interpreting God's will, since it is obvious that interpretations of the Ten Commandments vary and often conflict.

The most famous rule deontological theory was formulated by Immanuel Kant (1724-1804). According to Kant nothing is good in itself except a good will. The determining factor in any moral act, he argued, is the individual's intention or motive. While most of our everyday acts stem from emotional and habitual inclinations, or motives of self-interest, physical need, and whatever, only those acts can be considered moral which rest upon reason, will, and a sense of duty. Suppose that two people perform the same kind of act, resulting in similar consequences, but that the first person acts from self-interest, emotion, or habit, and the second acts from a sense of duty; according to Kant only the latter is morally praiseworthy. True moral worth stems from the recognition of one's duty and the choice to implement it.

But in any particular situation what is our duty, and

how can we know it? The answer to this is the keystone of Kant's moral system, his fundamental moral rule, the *Categorical Imperative*. Roughly stated, the Categorical Imperative says that in any given situation our duty is to act in such a way that we can also will that the maxim, or general rule, governing our action should become a universal law. The basic idea is that we should act in such a manner that upon reflection we can rationally and sincerely will that every other person in similar circumstances act in the same way. If we can do this and act accordingly, says Kant, we will have satisfied our moral obligation. There is a vague similarity between the Categorical Imperative and the Golden Rule, "Do unto others as you would have them do unto you."

While Kant's theory contains many positive features, accords well with common sense, and avoids the pitfalls of teleological views, there still are certain problems. There seems to be no clear way of resolving conflicts over moral judgments in cases where different persons categorically affirm opposing actions. The abortion question is a good example. One person might rationally and sincerely will that abortion under certain circumstances become a universal law; whereas someone else might equally will it to be a universal law that abortion never be allowed under any circumstances. It is unclear how Kant would deal with such moral disputes.

Another problem is that counter-examples can be given of actions which seem to have no moral worth at all and yet on Kant's scheme would be obligatory. Consider the action of brushing our teeth in the morning. This action is something which we will, and it seems to be the kind of action we could will to become a universal law. While it satisfies the conditions of the Categorical Imperative, we would hardly want to say that brushing our teeth every morning is a moral obligation.

In sum, having briefly discussed some of the major normative positions, we can draw only one conclusion: it is a difficult matter to choose among alternative theories. Teleological theories cannot escape the problem of how to compute the long-term consequences of a moral action. Act deontology seems too highly individualistic, lacking any means except intuition for justifying moral judgments. And rule deontology, whatever

form it takes, seems to provide for nc open discussion of
moral quandries, since by positing its rules it closes the
door by arbitrarily stating what is right and wrong. What,
then, are we to do? Perhaps what is needed is some synthesis
incorporating the best features of various systems while de-
leting the worst. In any case, the field of normative ethics
remains open.

W. T. STACE

ABSOLUTISM AND RELATIVISM

According to the absolutists there is but one eternally
true and valid moral code. This moral code applies with rigid
impartiality to all men. What is a duty for me must likewise
be a duty for you. And this will be true whether you are an
Englishman, a Chinaman, or a Hottentot. If cannibalism is an
abomination in England or America, it is an abomination in
central Africa, notwithstanding that the African may think
otherwise. The fact that he sees nothing wrong in his cannibal
practices does not make them for him morally right. They are
as much contrary to morality for him as they are for us. The
only difference is that he is an ignorant savage who does not
know this. There is not one law for one man or race of men,
another for another. There is not one moral standard for
Europeans, another for Indians, another for Chinese. There
is but one law, one standard, one morality, for all men. And
this standard, this law, is absolute and unvarying.

Moreover, as the one moral law extends its dominion over
all the corners of the earth, so too it is not limited in its
application by any considerations of time or period. That
which is right now was right in the centuries of Greece and
Rome, nay, in the very ages of the cave man. That which is
evil now was evil then. If slavery is morally wicked today,
it was morally wicked among the ancient Athenians, notwithstanding that their greatest men accepted it as a necessary
condition of human society. Their opinion did not make slavery a moral good for them. It only showed that they were, in

spite of their otherwise noble conceptions, ignorant of what is truly right and good in this matter.

The ethical absolutist recognizes as a fact that moral customs and moral ideas differ from country to country and from age to age. This indeed seems manifest and not to be disputed. We think slavery morally wrong, the Greeks thought it morally unobjectionable. The inhabitants of New Guinea certainly have very different moral ideas from ours. But the fact that the Greeks or the inhabitants of New Guinea think something right does not make it right, even for them. Nor does the fact that we think the same things wrong make them wrong. They are *in themselves* either right or wrong. What we have to do is to discover which they are. What anyone thinks makes no difference. It is here just as it is in matters of physical science. We believe the earth to be a globe. Our ancestors may have thought it flat. This does not show that it *was* flat, and is *now* a globe. What it shows is that men having in other ages been ignorant about the shape of the earth have now learned the truth. So if the Greeks thought slavery morally legitimate, this does not indicate that it was for them and in that age morally legitimate, but rather that they were ignorant of the truth of the matter.

. . .

. . . Now ethical absolutism was, in its central ideas, the product of Christian theology.

The connection is not difficult to detect. For morality has been conceived, during the Christian dispensation, as issuing from the will of God. That indeed was its single and all-sufficient source. There would be no point, for the naive believer in the faith, in the philosopher's questions regarding the foundations of morality and the basis of moral obligation. Even to ask such questions is a mark of incipient religious scepticism. For the true believer the author of the moral law is God. What pleases God, what God commands--that is the definition of right. What displeases God, what he forbids--that is the definition of wrong. Now there is, for the Christian monotheist, only one God ruling over the entire universe. And this God is rational, self-consistent. He does

116

not act upon whims. Consequently his will and his commands must be the same everywhere. They will be unvarying for all peoples and in all ages. If the heathen have other moral ideas than ours--inferior ideas--that can only be because they live in ignorance of the true God. If they knew God and his commands, their ethical precepts would be the same as ours.

. . .

We can now turn to the consideration of ethical relativity. . . . Ethical relativity is, in its essence, a purely negative creed. It is simply a denial of ethical absolutism. That is why the best way of explaining it is to begin by explaining ethical absolutism. If we understand that what the latter asserts the former denies, then we understand ethical relativity.

Any ethical position which denies that there is a single moral standard which is equally applicable to all men at all times may fairly be called a species of ethical relativity. There is not, the relativist asserts, merely one moral law, one code, one standard. There are many moral laws, codes, standards. What morality ordains in one place or age may be quite different from what morality ordains in another place or age. The moral code of Chinamen is quite different from that of Europeans, that of African savages quite different from both. Any morality, therefore, is relative to the age, the place, and the circumstances in which it is found. It is in no sense absolute.

This does not mean merely--as one might at first sight be inclined to suppose--that the very same kind of action which is *thought* right in one country and period may be *thought* wrong in another. This would be a mere platitude, the truth of which everyone would have to admit. Even the absolutist would admit this--would even wish to emphasize it--since he is well aware that different peoples have different sets of moral ideas, and his whole point is that some of these sets of ideas are false. What the relativist means to assert is, not this platitude, but that the very same kind of action which *is* right in one country and period may *be* wrong in another. And this, far from being a platitude, is a very startling assertion.

117

It is very important to grasp thoroughly the difference
between the two ideas. For there is reason to think that many
minds tend to find ethical relativity attractive because they
fail to keep them clearly apart. It is so very obvious that
moral ideas differ from country to country and from age to
age. And it is so very easy, if you are mentally lazy, to
suppose that to say this means the same as to say that no
universal moral standard exists,—or in other words that it
implies ethical relativity. We fail to see that the word
"standard" is used in two different senses. It is perfectly
true that, in one sense, there are many variable moral standards. We speak of judging a man by the standard of his time.
And this implies that different times have different standards.
And this, of course, is quite true. But when the word "standard" is used in this sense it means simply the set of moral
ideas current during the period in question. It means what
people *think* right, whether as a matter of fact it *is* right
or not. On the other hand when the absolutist asserts that
there exists a single universal moral "standard," he is not
using the word in this sense at all. He means by "standard"
what *is* right as distinct from what people merely think right.
His point is that although what people think right varies in
different countries and periods, yet what actually is right
is everywhere and always the same. And it follows that when
the ethical relativist disputes the position of the absolutist
and denies that any universal moral standard exists he too
means by "standard" what actually is right. But it is ex-
ceedingly easy, if we are not careful, to slip loosely from
using the word in the first sense to using it in the second
sense; and to suppose that the variability of moral beliefs
is the same thing as the variability of what really is moral.
And unless we keep the two senses of the word "standard" distinct, we are likely to think the creed of ethical relativity
much more plausible than it actually is.

The genuine relativist, then, does not merely mean that
Chinamen may think right what Frenchmen think wrong. He means
that what *is* wrong for the Frenchman may *be* right for the
Chinaman. And if one inquires how, in those circumstances,
one is to know what actually is right in China or in France,
the answer comes quite glibly. What is right in China is the
same as what people think right in China; and what is right

in France is the same as what people think right in France.
So that, if you want to know what is moral in any particular
country or age all you have to do is to ascertain what are
the moral ideas current in that age or country. Those ideas
are, *for that age or country*, right. Thus what is morally
right is identified with what is thought to be morally right,
and the distinction which we made above between these two is
simply denied. To put the same thing in another way, it is
denied that there can be or ought to be any distinction between the two senses of the word "standard." There is only
one kind of standard of right and wrong, namely, the moral
ideas current in any particular age or country.

Moral right *means* what people think morally right. It
has no other meaning. What Frenchmen think right is, therefore, right *for Frenchmen.* And evidently one must conclude--
though I am not aware that relativists are anxious to draw
one's attention to such unsavoury but yet absolutely necessary
conclusions from their creed--that cannibalism is right for
people who believe in it, that human sacrifice is right for
those races which practice it, and that burning widows alive
was right for Hindus until the British stepped in and compelled
the Hindus to behave immorally by allowing their widows to
remain alive.

When it is said that, according to the ethical relativist,
what is thought right in any social group is right for that
group, one must be careful not to misinterpret this. The relativist does not, of course, mean that there actually is an
objective moral standard in France and a different objective
standard in England, and that French and British opinions
respectively give us correct information about these different
standards. His point is rather that there are no objectively
true moral standards at all. There is no single universal
objective standard. Nor are there a variety of local objective standards. All standards are subjective. People's subjective feelings about morality are the only standards which
exist.

To sum up. The ethical relativist consistently denies,
it would seem, whatever the ethical absolutist asserts. For
the absolutist there is a single universal moral standard.
For the relativist there is no such standard. There are only

119

local, ephemeral, and variable standards. For the absolutist
there are two senses of the word "standard." Standards in the
sense of sets of current moral ideas are relative and change-
able. But the standard in the sense of what is actually morally right is absolute and unchanging. For the relativist no
such distinction can be made. There is only one meaning of
the word standard, namely, that which refers to local and
variable sets of moral ideas. Or if it is insisted that the
word must be allowed two meanings, then the relativist will
say that there is at any rate no actual example of a standard
in the absolute sense, and that the word as thus used is an
empty name to which nothing in reality corresponds; so that
the distinction between the two meanings becomes empty and
useless. Finally—though this is merely saying the same thing
in another way—the absolutist makes a distinction between
what actually is right and what is thought right. The relativist rejects this distinction and identifies what is moral
with what is thought moral by certain human beings or groups
of human beings.

G. E. MOORE

GOODNESS AS A SIMPLE PROPERTY

6. What, then, is good? How is good to be defined? Now, it may be thought that this is a verbal question. A definition does indeed often mean the expressing of one word's meaning in other words. But this is not the sort of definition I am asking for. Such a definition can never be of ultimate importance in any study except lexicography. If I wanted that kind of definition I should have to consider in the first place how people generally used the word 'good'; but my business is not with its proper usage, as established by custom. I should, indeed, be foolish, if I tried to use it for something which it did not usually denote: if, for instance, I were to announce that, whenever I used the word 'good', I must be understood to be thinking of that object which is usually denoted by the word 'table'. I shall, therefore, use the word in the sense in which I think it is ordinarily used; but at the same time I am not anxious to discuss whether I am right in thinking that it is so used. My business is solely with that object or idea, which I hold, rightly or wrongly, that the word is generally used to stand for. What I want to discover is the nature of that object or idea, and about this I am extremely anxious to arrive at an agreement.

But, if we understand the question in this sense, my answer to it may seem a very disappointing one. If I am asked 'What is good?' my answer is that good is good, and that is the end of the matter. Or if I am asked 'How is good to be defined?' my answer is that it cannot be defined, and that is all I have to say about it. But disappointing as these answers may appear, they are of the very last importance. . . .

From G. E. Moore, *Principia Ethica*, c 1929, chpt. I. Reprinted with permission by Cambridge University Press.

7. Let us, then, consider this position. My point is that 'good' is a simple notion, just as 'yellow' is a simple notion; that, just as you cannot, by any manner of means, explain to any one who does not already know it, what yellow is, so you cannot explain what good is. Definitions of the kind that I was asking for, definitions which describe the real nature of the object or notion denoted by a word, and which do not merely tell us what the word is used to mean, are only possible when the object or notion in question is something complex. You can give a definition of a horse, because a horse has many different properties and qualities, all of which you can enumerate. But when you have enumerated them all, when you have reduced a horse to his simplest terms, then you can no longer define those terms. They are simply something which you think of or perceive, and to any one who cannot think of or perceive them, you can never, by any definition, make their nature known. It may perhaps be objected to this that we are able to describe to others, objects which they have never seen or thought of. We can, for instance, make a man understand what a chimaera is, although he has never heard of one or seen one. You can tell him that it is an animal with a lioness's head and body, with a goat's head growing from the middle of its back, and with a snake in place of a tail. But here the object which you are describing is a complex object; it is entirely composed of parts, with which we are all perfectly familiar—a snake, a goat, a lioness; and we know, too, the manner in which those parts are to be put together, because we know what is meant by the middle of a lioness's back, and where her tail is wont to grow. And so it is with all objects, not previously known, which we are able to define: they are all complex; all composed of parts, which may themselves, in the first instance, be capable of similar definition, but which must in the end be reducible to simplest parts, which can no longer be defined. But yellow and good, we say, are not complex: they are notions of that simple kind, out of which definitions are composed and with which the power of further defining ceases.

10. 'Good', then, if we mean by it that quality which we assert to belong to a thing, when we say that the thing is good, is incapable of any definition, in the most important sense of that word. The most important sense of 'definition'

122

is that in which a definition states what are the parts which invariably compose a certain whole; and in this sense 'good' has no definition because it is simple and has no parts. It is one of those innumerable objects of thought which are themselves incapable of definition, because they are the ultimate terms by reference to which whatever *is* capable of definition must be defined. That there must be an indefinite number of such terms is obvious, on reflection; since we cannot define anything except by an analysis, which, when carried as far as it will go, refers us to something, which is simply different from anything else, and which by that ultimate difference explains the peculiarity of the whole which we are defining: for every whole contains some parts which are common to other wholes also. There is, therefore, no intrinsic difficulty in the contention that 'good' denotes a simple and indefinable quality. There are many other instances of such qualities.

13. In fact, if it is not the case that 'good' denotes something simple and indefinable, only two alternatives are possible: either it is a complex, a given whole, about the correct analysis of which there may be disagreement; or else it means nothing at all, and there is no such subject as Ethics. . . . Neither of these possibilities has, however, been clearly conceived and seriously maintained, as such, by those who presume to define good; and both may be dismissed by a simple appeal to facts.

(1) The hypothesis that disagreement about the meaning of good is disagreement with regard to the correct analysis of a given whole, may be most plainly seen to be incorrect by consideration of the fact that, whatever definition be offered, it may be always asked, with significance, of the complex so defined, whether it is itself good. To take, for instance, one of the more plausible, because one of the more complicated, of such proposed definitions, it may easily be thought, at first sight, that to be good may mean to be that which we desire to desire. Thus if we apply this definition to a particular instance, and say 'When we think that A is good, we are thinking that A is one of the things which we desire to desire', our proposition may seem quite plausible. But, if we carry the investigation further, and ask ourselves 'Is it good to desire to desire A?' it is apparent, on a little

reflection, that this question is itself as intelligible, as the original question 'Is A good?'—that we are, in fact, now asking for exactly the same information about the desire to desire A, for which we formerly asked with regard to A itself. But it is also apparent that the meaning of this second question cannot be correctly analysed into 'Is the desire to desire A one of the things which we desire to desire?': we have not before our minds anything so complicated as the question 'Do we desire to desire to desire to desire A?' Moreover any one can easily convince himself by inspection that the predicate of this proposition—'good'—is positively different from the notion of 'desiring to desire' which enters into its subject: 'That we should desire to desire A is good' is *not* merely equivalent to 'That A should be good is good'. It may indeed be true that what we desire to desire is always also good; perhaps, even the converse may be true: but it is very doubtful whether this is the case, and the mere fact that we understand very well what is meant by doubting it, shows clearly that we have two different notions before our minds.

(2) And the same consideration is sufficient to dismiss the hypothesis that 'good' has no meaning whatsoever. It is very natural to make the mistake of supposing that what is universally true is of such a nature that its negation would be self-contradictory: the importance which has been assigned to analytic propositions in the history of philosophy shows how easy such a mistake is. And thus it is very easy to conclude that what seems to be a universal ethical principle is in fact an identical proposition; that, if, for example, whatever is called 'good' seems to be pleasant, the proposition 'Pleasure is the good' does not assert a connection between two different notions, but involves only one, that of pleasure, which is easily recognised as a distinct entity. But whoever will attentively consider with himself what is actually before his mind when he asks the question 'Is pleasure (or whatever it may be) after all good?' can easily satisfy himself that he is not merely wondering whether pleasure is pleasant. And if he will try this experiment with each suggested definition in succession, he may become expert enough to recognise that in every case he has before his mind a unique object, with regard to the connection of which with any other object, a distinct question may be asked. Every one does in fact understand the

question 'Is this good?' When he thinks of it, his state of
mind is different from what it would be, were he asked 'Is
this pleasant, or desired, or approved?' It has a distinct
meaning for him, even though he may not recognise in what respect it is distinct. Whenever he thinks of 'intrinsic value',
or 'intrinsic worth', or says that a thing 'ought to exist',
he has before his mind the unique object—the unique property
of things—which I mean by 'good'. Everybody is constantly
aware of this notion, although he may never become aware at
all that it is different from other notions of which he is also
aware. But, for correct ethical reasoning, it is extremely
important that he should become aware of this fact; and, as
soon as the nature of the problem is clearly understood, there
should be little difficulty in advancing so far in analysis.

   'Good', then, is indefinable . . .

AN EMOTIVE THEORY OF ETHICS

One of the primary tasks of moral philosophy is to clarify the meaning of various ethical terms. When a person says of a certain action, "That is good," what actually is the meaning of 'good'? This same type of question arises in connection with the use of any and all other ethical concepts and symbols. This general problem of meaning has led to the somewhat recent development of the so-called "emotive theory of ethics," originally associated with the school of philosophy known as logical positivism, and most notably defended by C. L. Stevenson.[1] The following essay is intended as an exposition of the basic tenets of the emotive theory.

Let us begin by distinguishing three uses or functions of language: the reportive or assertive function, the expressive function, and the provocative or dynamic function. We often use language to make an assertion or report a fact. Thus we might say, "James was at the party last night," or, "It is a fact that water freezes at 32° F." It is only when language is used in this way that it can legitimately be asked whether what is said is *true* or *false*. Furthermore, it is only with reference to this reportive or assertive function of language that we can speak of *knowing* something; likewise of *verifying* whether something is or is not the case.

The expressive function of language is exemplified most obviously in emotional ejaculations, where the words we use

---

The present analysis is patterned after that offerred by A. J. Ayer, in *Language, Truth and Logic,* Chapt. VI.

[1]For reference see either of Stevenson's important works: *Facts and Values,* or *Ethics and Language.*

are meant purely to express our feelings. Upon receiving a
new car as a birthday present, we excitedly exclaim, "Wow!"
Our team scores a touchdown, we shout, "Hurrah!" Whereas we
bellow out "Boo!" when the referee makes a bad call against
our team. In many cases we express our feelings and emotions
by gestures rather than words: for example, by crying, by
laughing, by changing the tone of our voice, and by many other
ways. In each instance the meaning of the word or gesture or
tone of voice is nothing other than a reflection of our inner
feelings, an expression of our emotions. And just as truth
and falsehood do not apply to crying or laughing, it is plain
that the same holds for any statement which is purely emotive.
Indeed, one may question the sincerity of a person's emotions,
that is, whether or not the person actually has the feelings
which his statements or gestures express, but that is an entirely different matter than asking whether a given statement
is or is not true—the difference due to a difference in function.

The third function of language is its capacity to arouse
the feelings of others, to influence their attitudes, to provoke a change in their behavior, and to persuade them in a
given direction. Examples include commands ("Close the door.");
proposals ("Let's get married."); requests ("I wish you would
not play the TV so loud."); prescriptions ("You should brush
your teeth at least once a day."); and so on. In each case
the principle function of uttering the statement is to exert
an influence on the hearer, and to provoke the intended response on his part. Here, too, the notions of truth and falsehood are inappropriate. It just does not make sense to inquire
whether the statement "I recommend that you exercise more reg-
ularly" is true or false; such a statement simply is not used
in a cognitive manner.

Upon close inspection it becomes evident that the function
of ethical statements is purely 'emotive'—expressive and/or
provocative—never assertive. To begin with, the presence of
an ethical symbol in a given statement adds nothing to its
factual content. If I say to someone, "You acted wrongly in
not telling the truth," I am not reporting or asserting anything more than if I had simply said, "You did not tell the
truth." In adding that this action is wrong I am not making

127

a further report about it per se, but rather am expressing my
moral feelings (of disapproval) about the action. It is as
if I had said, "You did not tell the truth," in a peculiar tone
of admonishment, where the tone itself adds nothing to the lit-
eral meaning of the statement, but serves to express my attitude toward the action.

Suppose, now, that I generalize my previous statement and
write "Lying is wrong." This is a sentence that has no factual
meaning; that is, it neither reports nor asserts anything of
which we can legitimately ask whether it is true or false. I
could just as easily have written "Lying!!!"—where the exclamation marks might signify, by common consensus, that an attitude of moral disapproval is the feeling which is being expressed. Someone else may disagree with me regarding the
wrongness of lying, in the sense that he may not have the same
feelings about it as I do. We may even quarrel on account of
our opposing moral sentiments. However, in such a case of disagreement, there is no point in asking which of us is in the
right. Why? Because I am simply expressing my moral sentiments, and he is expressing his—but neither of us, strictly
speaking, is asserting a factual statement! Moral conflicts
are conflicts of attitudes, and attitudes are neither true nor
false.

We may conclude, therefore, that the meaning of ethical
terms is inextricably tied to their expressive function within
language. However, ethical statements usually serve a provocative function as well, in as much as they often are used to
arouse specific feelings in others and to provoke specific
types of action. Let's say I utter the sentence, "It is your
duty to tell the truth." This statement appears to have a
two-fold function: (1) to express my feelings toward telling
the truth, and (2) to exhort (prescribe or recommend that,
command, request) the listener to act accordingly, i.e. to
tell the truth. In this latter respect it is as if I had
uttered the command: "Tell the truth." Likewise, the sentence,
"You ought to tell the truth," involves the same type of exhortation, although here the tone of the command is less em-
phatic; whereas in the sentence, "It is good to tell the truth,"
the exhortation has become little more than a recommendation.
And herein lies the difference in meaning between the terms
'duty', 'ought', and 'good'.

128

In sum, we are able to clarify the meaning of ethical terms precisely in the degree to which we are able to decipher their emotive function(s) within language. Thus the sentence "X is good" might be understood as a kind of abbreviation for the multiple statement, "I approve of x; I recommend you do so also; act accordingly!" In no manner whatsoever is anything factual or objectively true being said about x, other than, of course, that I have morally positive feelings toward x, assuming here that I am being honest in expressing those feelings.

It is now clear that since ethical judgments do not serve an assertive function, there is no sense in asking whether a given moral judgment is true or false. As pure expressions of feeling, such statements simply do not come under the category of truth and falsehood. They are unverifiable for the same reason as a cry of pain, an exclamation of joy, or a word of command is unverifiable—because they do not assert any matter of fact.[1] Indeed, since moral statements are merely emotive expressions and provocative instruments of language, it follows that *there is no such thing as moral knowledge.* While it is perfectly proper to speak of moral attitudes and moral sentiments, and also personal differences in moral feelings, it is totally illegitimate—indeed, nonsensical—to speak of moral knowledge.

All of which leads to the recognition that there can be no such thing as ethical science, if by that one means the development of a 'true' system of morals. For the reasons previously mentioned, it is obvious that there is no way of

---

[1]Keep in mind the difference between *true* statements about something and *sincere* statements. Saying that a person is sincere in his statement is not the same as saying that his statement is true. For example, I might sincerely claim that "John was at the party last night," but my claim is not *true* unless in fact John was at the party. In the case of "X is good," if anything at all is being asserted—and that is debatable—it is certainly not *about x*, but *about the person* making the statement. And whatsoever knowledge is to be gained is psychological knowledge about the person's feelings—certainly not moral knowledge about x!

validating or verifying any ethical judgment or set of judgments, and no sense in asking whether any such judgments are
true. The only legitimate type of moral inquiry is the empirical investigation concerning the moral feelings and moral
habits of a given person or group of persons, a job entirely
within the scope of the social sciences.

CHAPTER FIVE

INVITATION TO EXISTENTIALISM

WHAT IS EXISTENTIALISM?

> *What is Truth but to live for an idea? . . . It is a question of discovering a truth which is truth for me, of finding the idea for which I am willing to live and die.*
>
> ---Søren Kierkegaard

Existentialism in the widest sense of the term is a philosophy having its emphasis on *concrete individual human existence.* What ultimately matters for the existentialist is the reality of human experience in all its facets: physical, emotional, and psychological. The focus is upon the individual person—with his distinctive qualities, goals, desires, emotions, joys and sufferings—rather than upon man in the abstract or the world in general. The underlying assumption in existentialist thought is that human existence cannot be reduced to a set of abstract concepts or be neatly defined by a series of scientific generalizations; on the contrary, human existence can be revealed only through concrete individual living experiences.

Existentialism finds expression not only in philosophy, but in theology, literature, and art as well. Some of the more prominent thinkers linked with existentialism include the religious writer Søren Kierkegaard (1813-1855), the nihilistic anti-philosopher Friedrich Nietzsche (1844-1900), the Jewish scholar Martin Buber (1878-1965), the Protestant theologian Paul Tillich (1886-1965), the Catholic social and moral philosopher Karl Jaspers (1883-1969), the atheistic humanist Jean-Paul Sartre (1905-   ), and such famous novelists as Fyodor Dostoyevsky (1821-1881), Franz Kafka (1883-1924), and Albert Camus (1913-1960).

133

Although they characteristically share a common concern
for the individual, for subjective experience, and for the
significance of personal freedom, existentialists often rad-
ically differ in their views. In this respect it has even
been said that there are as many existentialisms as there are
existentialists. The point to be made is that there is no
such thing as *the* existentialist philosophy. Rather than a
set of tenets or a distinctive theory, existentialism should
more aptly be described as an expression of deeply reflective
thought as existing individuals grope with the meaning of their
own lives.

In many ways existentialism can be viewed as a movement
of protest against certain features of traditional philosophy
and modern society. It is in part a revolt against Greek
rationalism and against 'systematic' or speculative philosophy
in general. Existentialists insist that theory must not be
divorced from practice, the vital problems of human existence
must not be subordinated to questions of logic, the individual
self must not be sacrificed in the pursuit of all-encompassing
impersonal world views, as in Plato's theory of abstract uni-
versals, Hegel's spiritual dialectic, even Einstein's theory
of relativity, or B. F. Skinner's behaviorism. Where Hegel
concludes that *the real is the rational,* Nietzsche defiantly
proclaims: "In everything one thing is impossible: rational-
ity."[1] Indeed, exclaims the existentialist, man is the most
real being, a being who must live the contradictions and predicaments of his own situation. Herein existentialist thought
represents a radical shift toward the emotional, intuitive,
and subjective, with a consequent reaction against the logical,
intellectual, and objective.

In a similar vein existentialism emerges as a revolt
against the impersonal and dehumanizing nature of modern society with its industrialism, departmentalization, ultra-
technology, and objectivating sciences. Existentialists see
man in danger of becoming a tool or an object, with no more
dignity than the machine he operates or the computer he

---

[1]Friedrich Nietzsche, *Thus Spoke Zarathustra,* in *The
Portable Nietzsche,* ed. and trans. by Walter Kaufmann (New
York: Viking Press, Inc., 1968), p. 278.

programs. Living in an age of mass transience, urbanization, and an accelerated pace of living, more and more an individual finds himself alone, lost among the masses, estranged from his socio-historical surroundings. Alienation and how to cope with it is a running theme throughout the writings of Kierkegaard, Nietzsche, and Sartre; and it is the central focus of Camus' famous novel, *The Stranger.*

One of the most recurring questions in existentialist thinking is that concerning the meaning of life. What is man? What is his final destiny? What is the purpose of human existence? Camus regards the question about the meaning of life the most urgent and most demanding question that each and every individual must wrestle with. Different existentialists respond to the question in different ways. Kierkegaard, for instance, proffers the view that a person's highest destiny is to enter into a faith relationship with God. On the other hand, such authors as Nietzsche, Sartre, and Camus operate on the hypothesis that there is no God and no transcendent meaning to life, and hence take the position that whatever meaning there is to a person's life is precisely that which he himself creates through his choices, acts, and attitudes.

The principle method of existentialism is that of reflection, the purpose being the description and elucidation of man's being-in-the-world. This is sometimes called the *phenomenological method,* referring to the philosophical movement known as phenomenology, which came into prominence through the writings of Edmund Husserl (1859-1938). The intention is to lay bare the primordial structures of human consciousness and experience.

Through such reflection existentialists are awakened to the many dimensions of human subjectivity. Attention is directed to man's inner life, with its moods, anxieties, and decisions. While persistently stressing the freedom, dignity, and worth of the individual, existentialists realistically address the many facets of human weakness and insecurity: fear, anxiety, guilt, loneliness, despair, finitude, and death are all dominant existential themes.

For the existentialist, how an individual responds to the challenges and stresses of his unique situation is a determination of his very being. To respond passively, to drift through life, submitting to the pressures of the time and following the inclinations of habit, to become manipulated by one's emotions, to allow one's life to be molded by outside forces—this is to live inauthentically! On the other hand, says the existentialist, authentic existence is exhibited through action, assertiveness, and total involvement. Symbols of existential authenticity range from Kierkegaard's knight of faith, to Nietzsche's superman, to Camus' Sisyphus-like defiant and rebellious absurd hero. In each instance, genuine individuality and selfhood is seen in terms of a passionate act of will. "To be," says Sartre, "is to do."

In spite of their often differing views, what unites all existentialists is the doctrine that man is free in the sense that he 'creates' himself through his goals, choices, and actions. Existentialism's conception of man is not of a being possessing a ready-made character, formed by hereditary, biological, and environmental factors, and developed in accordance with strict psychological laws. Neither is man conceived as being determined by a conflux of emotions which sweep over him like external forces. On the contrary, his emotions, his attitudes, his temperaments and habits are looked upon as the result of the way the individual has decided to relate himself to the world around him. Furthermore, it is declared, an individual is free at any time to make a new choice of himself, and thereby to remake his character or so-called 'nature'. This is what Sartre and others mean by saying that for man "existence precedes essence." An individual's essence is shaped by his decisions and actions, not by some predetermined makeup.

In sum, existentialism is a philosophy in search of the truth about human reality—its predicaments and contradictions, its individuality and uniqueness, its inherent subjectivity, its worth; in short, its meaning. And existentialism's ultimate thesis is that such truth can never be rationally grasped or adequately articulated through abstract concepts, but is the type of truth which must be lived and experienced to ever be known.

SØREN KIERKEGAARD

FAITH, PASSION, TRUTH: THE POSSIBILITY FOR A TELEOLOGICAL SUSPENSION OF THE ETHICAL

"And God tempted Abraham and said unto him, Take Isaac, thine only son, whom thou lovest, and get thee into the land of Moriah, and offer him there for a burnt offering upon the mountain which I will show thee."

It was early in the morning, Abraham arose betimes, he had the asses saddled, left his tent, and Isaac with him, but Sarah looked out of the window after them until they had passed down the valley and she could see them no more. They rode in silence for three days. On the morning of the fourth day Abraham said never a word, but he lifted up his eyes and saw Mount Moriah afar off. He left the young men behind and went alone with Isaac beside him up to the mountain. But Abraham said to himself, "I will not conceal from Isaac whither this course leads him." He stood still, he laid his hand upon the head of Isaac in benediction, and Isaac bowed to receive the blessing. And Abraham's face was fatherliness, his look was mild, his speech encouraging. But Isaac was unable to understand him, his soul could not be exalted; he embraced Abraham's knees, he fell at his feet imploringly, he begged for his young life, for the fair hope of his future, he called to mind the joy in Abraham's house, he called to mind the sorrow and loneliness. Then Abraham lifted up the boy, he walked with him by his side, and his talk was full of comfort and exhortation. But Isaac could not understand him. He climbed

---

From Søren Kierkegaard, *Fear and Trembling and The Sickness Unto Death*, trans. by Walter Lowrie (copyright 1941, 1954 by Princeton University Press; Princeton paperback, 1968), pp. 27, 31-37, 64, 65, 67, 69, 70, and 77. Reprinted by permission of Princeton University Press.

137

Mount Moriah, but Isaac could not understand him. Then for
an instant he turned away from him, and when Isaac again saw
Abraham's face it was changed, his glance was wild, his form
was horror. He seized Isaac by the throat, threw him to the
ground, and said, "Stupid boy, dost thou then suppose that I
am thy father? I am an idolater. Dost thou suppose that this
is God's bidding? No, it is my desire." Then Isaac trembled
and cried out in his terror, "O God in heaven, have compassion
upon me. God of Abraham, have compassion upon me. If I have
no father upon earth, be Thou my father!" But Abraham in a
low voice said to himself, "O Lord in heaven, I thank Thee.
After all it is better for him to believe that I am a monster,
rather than that he should lose faith in Thee."

. . .

By faith Abraham went out from the land of his fathers
and became a sojourner in the land of promise. He left one
thing behind, took one thing with him: he left his earthly
understanding behind and took faith with him—otherwise he
would not have wandered forth but would have thought this unreasonable. By faith he was a stranger in the land of promise, and there was nothing to recall what was dear to him,
but by its novelty everything tempted his soul to melancholy
yearning—and yet he was God's elect, in whom the Lord was
well pleased! Yea, if he had been disowned, cast off from
God's grace, he could have comprehended it better; but now it
was like a mockery of him and of his faith. There was in the
world one too who lived in banishment from the fatherland he
loved. He is not forgotten, nor his Lamentations when he
sorrowfully sought and found what he had lost. There is no
song of Lamentations by Abraham. It is human to lament, human
to weep with them that weep, but it is greater to believe,
more blessed to contemplate the believer.

By faith Abraham received the promise that in his seed
all races of the world would be blessed. Time passed, the
possibility was there, Abraham believed; time passed, it became unreasonable, Abraham believed. There was in the world
one who had an expectation, time passed, the evening drew
nigh, he was not paltry enough to have forgotten his expectation, therefore he too shall not be forgotten. Then he

sorrowed, and sorrow did not deceive him as life had done, it
did for him all it could, in the sweetness of sorrow he possessed his delusive expectation. It is human to sorrow, human
to sorrow with them that sorrow, but it is greater to believe,
more blessed to contemplate the believer. There is no song of
Lamentations by Abraham. He did not mournfully count the days
while time passed, he did not look at Sarah with a suspicious
glance, wondering whether she were growing old, he did not
arrest the course of the sun, that Sarah might not grow old,
and his expectation with her. He did not sing lullingly before Sarah his mournful lay. Abraham became old, Sarah became
a laughingstock in the land, and yet he was God's elect and
inheritor of the promise that in his seed all the races of the
world would be blessed. So were it not better if he had not
been God's elect? What is it to be God's elect? It is to be
denied in youth the wishes of youth, so as with great pains to
get them fulfilled in old age. If Abraham had wavered, he
would have given it up. If he had said to God, "Then perhaps
it is not after all Thy will that it should come to pass, so
I will give up the wish. It was my only wish, it was my bliss.
My soul is sincere, I hide no secret malice because Thou didst
deny it to me"--he would not have been forgotten, he would
have saved many by his example, yet he would not be the father
of faith. For it is great to give up one's wish, but it is
greater to hold it fast after having given it up, it is great
to grasp the eternal, but it is greater to hold fast to the
temporal after having given it up.

      Then came the fulness of time. If Abraham had not be-
lieved, Sarah surely would have been dead of sorrow, and
Abraham, dulled by grief, would not have understood the fulfilment but would have smiled at it as at a dream of youth.
But Abraham believed, therefore he was young; for he who always hopes for the best becomes old, and he who is always pre-
pared for the worst grows old early, but he who believes pre-
serves an eternal youth. Praise therefore to that story! For
Sarah, though stricken in years, was young enough to desire
the pleasure of motherhood, and Abraham, though gray-haired,
was young enough to wish to be a father. In an outward respect the marvel consists in the fact that it came to pass
according to their expectation, in a deeper sense the miracle
of faith consists in the fact that Abraham and Sarah were
young enough to wish, and that faith had preserved their wish

and therewith their youth. He accepted the fulfilment of the promise, he accepted it by faith, and it came to pass according to the promise and according to his faith—for Moses smote the rock with his rod, but he did not believe.

Then there was joy in Abraham's house, when Sarah became a bride on the day of their golden wedding.

But it was not to remain thus. Still once more Abraham was to be tried. He had fought with that cunning power which invents everything, with that alert enemy which never slumbers, with that old man who outlives all things—he had fought with Time and preserved his faith. Now all the terror of the strife was concentrated in one instant. "And God tempted Abraham and said unto him, Take Isaac, thine only son, whom thou lovest, and get thee into the land of Moriah, and offer him there for a burnt offering upon the mountain which I will show thee."

So all was lost—more dreadfully than if it had never come to pass! So the Lord was only making sport of Abraham! He made miraculously the preposterous actual, and now in turn He would annihilate it. It was indeed foolishness, but Abraham did not laugh at it like Sarah when the promise was announced. All was lost! Seventy years of faithful expectation, the brief joy at the fulfilment of faith. Who then is he that plucks away the old man's staff, who is it that requires that he himself shall break it? Who is he that would make a man's gray hairs comfortless, who is it that requires that he himself shall do it? Is there no compassion for the venerable oldling, none for the innocent child? And yet Abraham was God's elect, and it was the Lord who imposed the trial. All would now be lost. The glorious memory to be preserved by the human race, the promise in Abraham's seed—this was only a whim, a fleeting thought which the Lord had had, which Abraham should now obliterate. That glorious treasure which was just as old as faith in Abraham's heart, many, many years older than Isaac, the fruit of Abraham's life, sanctified by prayers, matured in conflict—the blessing upon Abraham's lips, this fruit was now to be plucked prematurely and remain without significance. For what significance had it when Isaac was to be sacrificed? That sad and yet blissful hour when Abraham was to take leave of all that was dear to him, when

140

yet once more he was to lift up his head, when his countenance
would shine like that of the Lord, when he would concentrate
his whole soul in a blessing which was potent to make Isaac
blessed all his days--this time would not come! For he would
indeed take leave of Isaac, but in such a way that he himself
would remain behind; death would separate them, but in such a
way that Isaac remained its prey. The old man would not be
joyful in death as he laid his hands in blessing upon Isaac,
but he would be weary of life as he laid violent hands upon
Isaac. And it was God who tried him. Yea, woe, woe unto the
messenger who had come before Abraham with such tidings! Who
would have ventured to be the emissary of this sorrow? But it
was God who tried Abraham.

    Yet Abraham believed, and believed for this life. Yea,
if his faith had been only for a future life, he surely would
have cast everything away in order to hasten out of this world
to which he did not belong. But Abraham's faith was not of
this sort, if there be such a faith; for really this is not
faith but the furthest possibility of faith which has a pre-
sentiment of its object at the extremest limit of the horizon,
yet is separated from it by a yawning abyss within which despair carries on its game. But Abraham believed precisely for
this life, that he was to grow old in the land, honored by the
people, blessed in his generation, remembered forever in Isaac,
his dearest thing in life, whom he embraced with a love for
which it would be a poor expression to say that he loyally
fulfilled the father's duty of loving the son, as indeed is
evinced in the words of the summons, "the son whom thou lovest."
Jacob had twelve sons, and one of them he loved; Abraham had
only one, the son whom he loved.

    Yet Abraham believed and did not doubt, he believed the
preposterous. If Abraham had doubted--then he would have done
something else, something glorious; for how could Abraham do
anything but what is great and glorious! He would have marched
up to Mount Moriah, he would have cleft the fire-wood, lit the
pyre, drawn the knife--he would have cried out to God, "Despise
not this sacrifice, it is not the best thing I possess, that I
know well, for what is an old man in comparison with the child
of promise; but it is the best I am able to give Thee. Let
Isaac never come to know this, that he may console himself
with his youth." He would have plunged the knife into his own

141

breast. He would have been admired in the world, and his name would not have been forgotten; but it is one thing to be admired, and another to be the guiding star which saves the anguished.

But Abraham believed. He did not pray for himself, with the hope of moving the Lord—it was only when the righteous punishment was decreed upon Sodom and Gomorrha that Abraham came forward with his prayers.

We read in those holy books: "And God tempted Abraham, and said unto him, Abraham, Abraham, where are thou? And he said, Here am I." Thou to whom my speech is addressed, was such the case with thee? When afar off thou didst see the heavy dispensation of providence approaching thee, didst thou not say to the mountains, Fall on me, and to the hills, Cover me? Or if thou wast stronger, did not thy foot move slowly along the way, longing as it were for the old path? When a call was issued to thee, didst thou answer, or didst thou not answer perhaps in a low voice, whisperingly? Not so Abraham: joyfully, buoyantly, confidently, with a loud voice, he answered, "Here am I." We read further: "And Abraham rose early in the morning"—as though it were to a festival, so he hastened, and early in the morning he had come to the place spoken of, to Mount Moriah. He said nothing to Sarah, nothing to Eleazar. Indeed who could understand him? Had not the temptation by its very nature exacted of him an oath of silence? He cleft the wood, he bound Isaac, he lit the pyre, he drew the knife. My hearer, there was many a father who believed that with his son he lost everything that was dearest to him in the world, that he was deprived of every hope for the future, but yet there was none that was the child of promise in the sense that Isaac was for Abraham. There was many a father who lost his child; but then it was God, it was the unalterable, the unsearchable will of the Almighty, it was His hand took the child. Not so with Abraham. For him was reserved a harder trial, and Isaac's fate was laid along with the knife in Abraham's hand. And there he stood, the old man, with his only hope! But he did not doubt, he did not look anxiously to the right or to the left, he did not challenge heaven with his prayers. He knew that it was God the Almighty who was trying him, he knew that it was the hardest sacrifice

142

that could be required of him; but he knew also that no sacrifice was too hard when God required it—and he drew the knife.

Who gave strength to Abraham's arm? Who held his right
hand up so that it did not fall limp at his side? He who gazes
at this becomes paralyzed. Who gave strength to Abraham's
soul, so that his eyes did not grow dim, so that he saw neither
Isaac nor the ram? He who gazes at this becomes blind.—And
yet rare enough perhaps is the man who becomes paralyzed and
blind, still more rare one who worthily recounts what happened. We all know it—it was only a trial.

If Abraham when he stood upon Mount Moriah had doubted,
if he had gazed about him irresolutely, if before he drew the
knife he had by chance discovered the ram, if God had permitted
him to offer it instead of Isaac—then he would have betaken
himself home, everything would have been the same, he has
Sarah, he retained Isaac, and yet how changed! For his retreat
would have borne witness neither to his faith nor to God's
grace, but would have testified only how dreadful it is to
march out to Mount Moriah. Then Abraham would not have been
forgotten, nor would Mount Moriah, this mountain would then
be mentioned, not like Ararat where the Ark landed, but would
be spoken of as a consternation, because it was here that
Abraham doubted.

• • •

Is there such a thing as a teleological suspension of the ethical?

The ethical as such is the universal, and as the universal
it applies to everyone, which may be expressed from another
point of view by saying that it applies every instant. It re-
poses immanently in itself, it has nothing without itself which
is its *telos*, but is itself *telos* for everything outside it,
and when this has been incorporated by the ethical it can go
no further. Conceived immediately as physical and psychical,
the particular individual is the individual who has his *telos*
in the universal, and his ethical task is to express himself
constantly in it, to abolish his particularity in order to become the universal. As soon as the individual would assert
himself in his particularity over against the universal he

143

sins, and only by recognizing this can he again reconcile himself with the universal.

. . .

For faith is this paradox, that the particular is higher than the universal—yet in such a way, be it observed, that the movement repeats itself, and that consequently the individual, after having been in the universal, now as the particular isolates himself as higher than the universal. If this be not faith, then Abraham is lost, then faith has never existed in the world.

. . .

Abraham's relation to Isaac, ethically speaking, is quite simply expressed by saying that a father shall love his son more dearly than himself. Yet within its own compass the ethical has various gradations. Let us see whether in this story there is to be found any higher expression for the ethical such as would ethically explain his conduct, ethically justify him in suspending the ethical obligation toward his son, without in this search going beyond the teleology of the ethical.

. . .

The difference between the tragic hero and Abraham is clearly evident. The tragic hero still remains within the ethical. He lets one expression of the ethical find its *telos* in a higher expression of the ethical; the ethical relation between father and son, or daughter and father, he reduces to a sentiment which has its dialectic in its relation to the idea of morality. Here there can be no question of a teleological suspension of the ethical itself.

With Abraham the situation was different. By his act he overstepped the ethical entirely and possessed a higher *telos* outside of it, in relation to which he suspended the former. For I should very much like to know how one would bring Abraham's act into relation with the universal, and whether it is possible to discover any connection whatever between what Abraham did and the universal . . . except the fact that he transgressed it. It was not for the sake of saving a

144

people, not to maintain the idea of the state, that Abraham did this, and not in order to reconcile angry deities. If there could be a question of the deity being angry, he was angry only with Abraham, and Abraham's whole action stands in no relation to the universal, is a purely private undertaking. Therefore, whereas the tragic hero is great by reason of his moral virtue, Abraham is great by reason of a purely personal virtue. In Abraham's life there is no higher expression for the ethical than this, that the father shall love his son. Of the ethical in the sense of morality there can be no question in this instance. In so far as the universal was present, it was indeed cryptically present in Isaac, hidden as it were in Isaac's loins, and must therefore cry out with Isaac's mouth, "Do it not! Thou art bringing everything to naught."

Why then did Abraham do it? For God's sake, and (in complete identity with this) for his own sake. He did it for God's sake because God required this proof of his faith; for his own sake he did it in order that he might furnish the proof. The unity of these two points of view is perfectly expressed by the word which has always been used to characterize this situation: it is a trial, a temptation (*Fristelse*). A temptation—but what does that mean? What ordinarily tempts a man is that which would keep him from doing his duty, but in this case the temptation is itself the ethical . . . which would keep him from doing God's will. But what then is duty? Duty is precisely the expression for God's will.

. . .

The story of Abraham contains therefore a teleological suspension of the ethical. As the individual he became higher than the universal. This is the paradox which does not permit of mediation. It is just as inexplicable how he got into it as it is inexplicable how he remained in it. If such is not the position of Abraham, then he is not even a tragic hero but a murderer. To want to continue to call him the father of faith, to talk of this to people who do not concern themselves with anything but words, is thoughtless. A man can become a tragic hero by his own powers—but not a knight of faith. When a man enters upon the way, in a certain sense the hard way of the tragic hero, many will be able to give him counsel; to him who follows the narrow way of faith no one can give counsel,

145

him no one can understand. Faith is a miracle, and yet no
man is excluded from it; for that in which all human life is
unified is passion, and faith is a passion.

JEAN-PAUL SARTRE

FREEDOM AND RESPONSIBILITY

The essential consequence of our earlier remarks is that man being condemned to be free carries the weight of the whole world on his shoulders; he is responsible for the world and for himself as a way of being. We are taking the word "responsibility" in its ordinary sense as "consciousness (of) being the incontestable author of an event or of an object." In this sense the responsibility of /an individual7 is overwhelming since he is the one by whom it happens that *there is* a world; since he is also the one who makes himself be, then whatever may be the situation in which he finds himself, /he7 must wholly assume this situation with its peculiar coefficient of adversity, even though it be insupportable. He must assume the situation with the proud consciousness of being the author of it, for the very worst disadvantages or the worst threats which can endanger my person have meaning only in and through my project; and it is on the ground of the engagement which I am that they appear. It is therefore senseless to think of complaining since nothing foreign has decided what we feel, what we live, or what we are.

Furthermore this absolute responsibility is not resignation; it is simply the logical requirement of the consequences of our freedom. What happens to me happens through me, and I can neither affect myself with it nor revolt against it nor resign myself to it. Moreover everything which happens to me is *mine*. By this we must understand first of all that I am always equal to what happens to me *qua* man, for what happens

---

From Jean-Paul Sartre, *Being and Nothingness: An Essay on Phenomenological Ontology*, trans. by Hazel Barnes (New York: Philosophical Library, 1956), pp. 553-556. Reprinted by permission of the publisher.

147

to a man through other men and through himself can be only
human. The most terrible situations of war, the worst tor-
tures do not create a non-human state of things; there is no
non-human situation. It is only through fear, flight, and
recourse to magical types of conduct that I shall decide on
the non-human, but this decision is human, and I shall carry
the entire responsibility for it. But in addition the situation is *mine* because it is the image of my free choice of myself, and everything which it presents to me is *mine* in that
this represents me and symbolizes me. Is it not I who decide
the coefficient of adversity in things and even their unpre-
dictability by deciding myself?

Thus there are no accidents in a life; a community event
which suddenly bursts forth and involves me in it does not
come from the outside. If I am mobilized in a war, this war
is my war; it is in my image and I deserve it. I deserve it
first because I could always get out of it by suicide or by
desertion; these ultimate possibles are those which must always
be present for us when there is a question of envisaging a situation. For lack of getting out of it, I have chosen it. This
can be due to inertia, to cowardice in the face of public opinion, or because I prefer certain other values to the value of
the refusal to join in the war (the good opinion of my rela-
tives, the honor of my family, etc.). Anyway you look at it,
it is a matter of a choice. This choice will be repeated later
on again and again without a break until the end of the war.
Therefore we must agree with the statement by J. Romains, "In
war there are no innocent victims."[1] If therefore I have preferred war to death or to dishonor, everything takes place as
if I bore the entire responsibility for this war. Of course
others have declared it, and one might be tempted perhaps to
consider me as a simple accomplice. But this notion of com-
plicity has only a juridical sense, and it does not hold here.
For it depended on me that for me and by me this war should
not exist, and I have decided that it does exist. There was
no compulsion here, for the compulsion could have got no hold
on a freedom. I did not have any excuse; for as we have said
repeatedly, ... the peculiar character of human-reality is
that it is without excuse. Therefore it remains for me only

_____

[1]J. Romains: *Les hommes de bonne volonté*; "Prelude à Verdun."

to lay claim to this war.

But in addition the war is *mine* because by the sole fact that it arises in a situation which I cause to be and that I can discover it there only by engaging myself for or against it, I can no longer distinguish at present the choice which I make of myself from the choice which I make of the war. To live this war is to choose myself through it and to choose it through my choice of myself. There can be no question of considering it as "four years of vacation" or as a "reprieve," as a "recess," the essential part of my responsibilities being elsewhere in my married, family, or professional life. In this war which I have chosen I choose myself from day to day, and I make it mine by making myself. If it is going to be four empty years, then it is I who bear the responsibility for this.

Finally, as we pointed out earlier, each person is an absolute choice of self from the standpoint of a world of knowledges and of techniques which this choice both assumes and illumines; each person is an absolute upsurge at an absolute date and is perfectly unthinkable at another date. It is therefore a waste of time to ask what I should have been if this war had not broken out, for I have chosen myself as one of the possible meanings of the epoch which imperceptibly led to war. I am not distinct from this same epoch; I could not be transported to another epoch without contradiction. Thus *I am* this war which restricts and limits and makes comprehensible the period which preceded it. In this sense we may define more precisely the responsibility of the /Individual7 if to the earlier quoted statement, "There are no innocent victims," we add the words, "We have the war we deserve." Thus, totally free, undistinguishable from the period for which I have chosen to be the meaning, as profoundly responsible for the war as if I had myself declared it, unable to live without integrating it in *my* situation, engaging myself in it wholly and stamping it with my seal, I must be without remorse or regrets as I am without excuse; for from the instant of my upsurge into being, I carry the weight of the world by myself alone without anything or any person being able to lighten it.

Yet this responsibility is of a very particular type. Someone will say, "I did not ask to be born." This is a naive

149

way of throwing greater emphasis on our facticity. I am responsible for everything, in fact, except for my very responsibility, for I am not the foundation of my being. Therefore everything takes place as if I were compelled to be responsible. I am *abandoned* in the world, not in the sense that I might remain abandoned and passive in a hostile universe like a board floating on the water, but rather in the sense that I find myself suddenly alone and without help, engaged in a world for which I bear the whole responsibility without being able, whatever I do, to tear myself away from this responsibility for an instant. For I am responsible for my very desire of fleeing responsibilities. To make myself passive in the world, to refuse to act upon things and upon Others is still to choose myself, and suicide is one mode among others of being-in-the-world. Yet I find an absolute responsibility for the fact that my facticity (here the fact of my birth) is directly inapprehensible and even inconceivable, for this fact of my birth never appears as a brute fact but always across a projective reconstruction. . . . I am ashamed of being born or I am astonished at it or I rejoice over it, or in attempting to get rid of my life I affirm that I live and I assume this life as bad. Thus in a certain sense I *choose* being born. This choice itself is integrally affected with facticity since I am not able not to choose, but this facticity in turn will appear only in so far as I surpass it toward my ends. Thus facticity is everywhere but inapprehensible; I never encounter anything except my responsibility. That is why I can not ask, "Why was I born?" or curse the day of my birth or declare that I did not ask to be born, for these various attitudes toward my birth—i.e., toward the *fact* that I realize a presence in the world—are absolutely nothing else but ways of assuming this birth in full responsibility and of making it *mine*. Here again I encounter only myself and my projects so that finally my abandonment—i.e., my facticity—consists simply in the fact that I am condemned to be wholly responsible for myself.

. . . The one who realizes in anguish his condition as being thrown into a responsibility which extends to his very abandonment has no longer either remorse or regret or excuse; he is no longer anything but a freedom which perfectly reveals itself and whose being resides in this very revelation.

JEAN-PAUL SARTRE

BAD FAITH: FLIGHT FROM FREEDOM

We say indifferently of a person that he shows signs of
bad faith or that he lies to himself. We shall willingly grant
that bad faith is a lie to oneself, on condition that we distinguish the lie to oneself from lying in general. . . .

. . . To be sure, the one who practices bad faith is hiding a displeasing truth or presenting as truth a pleasing un-
truth. Bad faith then has in appearance the structure of
falsehood. Only what changes everything is the fact that in
bad faith it is from myself that I am hiding the truth. Thus
the duality of the deceiver and the deceived does not exist
here.

. . .

Take the example of a woman who has consented to go out
with a particular man for the first time. She knows very well
the intentions which the man who is speaking to her cherishes
regarding her. She knows also that it will be necessary sooner
or later for her to make a decision. But she does not want to
realize the urgency; she concerns herself only with what is
respectful and discreet in the attitude of her companion. She
does not apprehend this conduct as an attempt to achieve what
we call "the first approach"; that is, she does not want to
see possibilities of temporal development which his conduct
presents. She restricts this behavior to what is in the present; she does not wish to read in the phrases which he

---

From Jean-Paul Sartre, *Being and Nothingness: An Essay
on Phenomenological Ontology,* trans. by Hazel Barnes (New York:
Philosophical Library, 1956), pp. 48-49, 55-56. Reprinted by
permission of the publisher.

addresses to her anything other than their explicit meaning. If he says to her, "I find you so attractive!" she disarms this phrase of its sexual background; she attaches to the conversation and to the behavior of the speaker, the immediate meanings, which she imagines as objective qualities. The man who is speaking to her appears to her sincere and respectful as the table is round or square, as the wall coloring is blue or gray. The qualities thus attached to the person she is listening to are in this way fixed in a permanence like that of things, which is no other than the projection of the strict present of the qualities into the temporal flux. This is because she does not quite know what she wants. She is profoundly aware of the desire which she inspires, but the desire cruel and naked would humiliate and horrify her. Yet she would find no charm in a respect which would be only respect. In order to satisfy her, there must be a feeling which is addressed wholly to her *personality*—i.e., to her full freedom—and which would be a recognition of her freedom. But at the same time this feeling must be wholly desire; that is, it must address itself to her body as object. This time then she refuses to apprehend the desire for what it is; she does not even give it a name; she recognizes it only to the extent that it transcends itself toward admiration, esteem, respect and that it is wholly absorbed in the more refined forms which it produces, to the extent of no longer figuring anymore as a sort of warmth and density. But then suppose he takes her hand. This act of her companion risks changing the situation by calling for an immediate decision. To leave the hand there is to consent in herself to flirt, to engage herself. To withdraw it is to break the troubled and unstable harmony which gives the hour its charm. The aim is to postpone the moment of decision as long as possible. We know what happens next; the young woman leaves her hand there, but she *does not notice* that she is leaving it. She does not notice because it happens by chance that she is at this moment all intellect. She draws her companion up to the most lofty regions of sentimental speculation; she speaks of Life, of her life, she shows herself in her essential aspect—a personality, a consciousness. And during this time the divorce of the body from the soul is accomplished; the hand rests inert between the warm hands of her companion—neither consenting nor resisting—a thing. *We shall say that this woman is in bad faith.*

ALBERT CAMUS

ABSURD MAN

ABSURDITY AND SUICIDE

There is but one truly serious philosophical problem, and
that is suicide. Judging whether life is or is not worth living
amounts to answering the fundamental question of philosophy.
All the rest—whether or not the world has three dimensions,
whether the mind has nine or twelve categories—comes afterwards. These are games; one must first answer. And if it is
true, as Nietzsche claims, that a philosopher, to deserve our
respect, must preach by example, you can appreciate the importance of that reply, for it will precede the definitive act.
These are facts the heart can feel; yet they call for careful
study before they become clear to the intellect.

If I ask myself how to judge that this question is more
urgent than that, I reply that one judges by the actions it
entails. I have never seen anyone die for the ontological
argument. Galileo, who held a scientific truth of great importance, abjured it with the greatest ease as soon as it en-
dangered his life. In a certain sense, he did right. That
truth was not worth the stake. Whether the earth or the sun
revolves around the other is a matter of profound indifference.
To tell the truth, it is a futile question. On the other hand,
I see many people die because they judge that life is not worth
living. I see others paradoxically getting killed for the
ideas or illusions that give them a reason for living (what is
called a reason for living is also an excellent reason for dying). I therefore conclude that the meaning of life is the

---

most urgent of questions.

. . . In a sense, and as in melodrama, killing yourself
amounts to confessing. It is confessing that life is too much
for you or that you do not understand it. Let's not go too
far in such analogies, however, but rather return to everyday
words. It is merely confessing that that "is not worth the
trouble." Living, naturally, is never easy. You continue
making the gestures commanded by existence for many reasons,
the first of which is habit. Dying voluntarily implies that
you have recognized, even instinctively, the ridiculous character of that habit, the absence of any profound reason for
living, the insane character of that daily agitation, and the
uselessness of suffering.

. . . Hitherto,and it has not been wasted effort, people
have played on words and pretended to believe that refusing
to grant a meaning to life necessarily leads to declaring that
it is not worth living. In truth, there is no necessary common measure between these two judgments. One merely has to
refuse to be misled by the confusions, divorces, and incon-
sistencies previously pointed out. One must brush everything
aside and go straight to the real problem. One kills oneself
because life is not worth living, that is certainly a truth—
yet an unfruitful one because it is a truism. But does that
insult to existence, that flat denial in which it is plunged
come from the fact that it has no meaning? Does its absurdity
require one to escape it through hope or suicide—this is what
must be clarified, hunted down, and elucidated while brushing
aside all the rest. Does the Absurd dictate death?

THE MYTH OF SISYPHUS

The gods had condemned Sisyphus to ceaselessly rolling a
rock to the top of a mountain, whence the stone would fall
back of its own weight. They had thought with some reason
that there is no more dreadful punishment than futile and hope-
less labor.

If one believes Homer, Sisyphus was the wisest and most
prudent of mortals. According to another tradition, however,
he was disposed to practice the profession of highwayman. I
see no contradiction in this. Opinions differ as to why he

154

became the futile laborer of the underworld. To begin with, he is accused of a certain levity in regard to the gods. He stole their secrets. Aegina, the daughter of Aesopus, was carried off by Jupiter. The father was shocked by that disappearance and complained to Sisyphus. He, who knew of the abduction, offered to tell about it on condition that Aesopus would give water to the citadel of Corinth. To the celestial thunderbolts he preferred the benediction of water. He was punished for this in the underworld. Homer tells us also that Sisyphus had put Death in chains. Pluto could not endure the sight of his deserted, silent empire. He dispatched the god of war, who liberated Death from the hands of her conqueror.

It is said also that Sisyphus, being near to death, rashly wanted to test his wife's love. He ordered her to cast his unburied body into the middle of the public square. Sisyphus woke up in the underworld. And there, annoyed by an obedience so contrary to human love, he obtained from Pluto permission to return to earth in order to chastise his wife. But when he had seen again the face of this world, enjoyed water and sun, warm stones and the sea, he no longer wanted to go back to the infernal darkness. Recalls, signs of anger, warnings were of no avail. Many years more he lived facing the curve of the gulf, the sparkling sea, and the smiles of earth. A decree of the gods was necessary. Mercury came and seized the impudent man by the collar and, snatching him from his joys, led him forcibly back to the underworld, where his rock was ready for him.

You have already grasped that Sisyphus is the absurd hero. He *is*, as much through his passions as through his torture. His scorn of the gods, his hatred of death, and his passion for life won him that unspeakable penalty in which the whole being is exerted toward accomplishing nothing. This is the price that must be paid for the passions of this earth. Nothing is told us about Sisyphus in the underworld. Myths are made for the imagination to breathe life into them. As for this myth, one sees merely the whole effort of a body straining to raise the huge stone, to roll it and push it up a slope a hundred times over; one sees the face screwed up, the cheek tight against the stone, the shoulder bracing the clay-covered mass, the foot wedging it, the fresh start with arms outstretched, the wholly human security of two earth-clotted hands. At the very end of his long effort measured by skyless space and time without depth, the purpose is achieved. Then Sisyphus watches the stone rush down in a few moments toward that lower world whence he will have to push it up again toward the summit. He goes back down to the plain.

It is during that return, that pause, that Sisyphus interests me. A face that toils so close to stones is already stone itself! I see that man going back down with a heavy yet measured step toward the torment of which he will never know the end. That hour like a breathing-space which returns as surely as his suffering, that is the hour of consciousness. At each of those moments when he leaves the heights and gradually sinks toward the lairs of the gods, he is superior to his fate. He is stronger than his rock.

If this myth is tragic, that is because its hero is conscious. Where would his torture be, indeed, if at every step the hope of succeeding upheld him? The workman of today works every day in his life at the same tasks, and this fate is no less absurd. But it is tragic only at the rare moments when it becomes conscious. Sisyphus, proletarian of the gods, powerless and rebellious, knows the whole extent of his wretched condition: it is what he thinks of during his descent. The lucidity that was to constitute his torture at the same time crowns his victory. There is no fate that cannot be surmounted by scorn.

If the descent is thus sometimes performed in sorrow, it can also take place in joy. This word is not too much. Again I fancy Sisyphus returning toward his rock, and the sorrow was in the beginning. When the images of earth cling too tightly to memory, when the call of happiness becomes too insistent, it happens that melancholy rises in man's heart: this is the rock's victory, this is the rock itself. The boundless grief is too heavy to bear. These are our nights of Gethsemane. But crushing truths perish from being acknowledged. Thus, Oedipus at the outset obeys fate without knowing it. But from the moment he knows, his tragedy begins. Yet at the same moment, blind and desperate, he realizes that the only bond linking

156

him to the world is the cool hand of a girl. Then a tremen-
dous remark rings out: "Despite so many ordeals, my advanced
age and the nobility of my soul make me conclude that all is
well." Sophocles' Oedipus, like Dostoevsky's Kirilov, thus
gives the recipe for the absurd victory. Ancient wisdom con-
firms modern heroism.

One does not discover the absurd without being tempted
to write a manual of happiness. "What! by such narrow ways--?"
There is but one world, however. Happiness and the absurd are
two sons of the same earth. They are inseparable. It would
be a mistake to say that happiness necessarily springs from
the absurd discovery. It happens as well that the feeling of
the absurd springs from happiness. "I conclude that all is
well," says Oedipus, and that remark is sacred. It echoes in
the wild and limited universe of man. It teaches that all is
not, has not been, exhausted. It drives out of this world a
god who had come into it with dissatisfaction and a preference
for futile sufferings. It makes of fate a human matter, which
must be settled among men.

All Sisyphus' silent joy is contained therein. His fate
belongs to him. His rock is his thing. Likewise, the absurd
man, when he contemplates his torment, silences all the idols.
In the universe suddenly restored to its silence, the myriad
wondering little voices of the earth rise up. Unconscious,
secret calls, invitations from all the faces, they are the
necessary reverse and price of victory. There is no sun without shadow, and it is essential to know the night. The absurd
man says yes and his effort will henceforth be unceasing. If
there is a personal fate, there is no higher destiny, or at
least there is but one which he concludes is inevitable and
despicable. For the rest, he knows himself to be the master
of his days. At that subtle moment when man glances backward
over his life, Sisyphus returning toward his rock, in that
slight pivoting he contemplates that series of unrelated actions which becomes his fate, created by him, combined under
his memory's eye and soon sealed by his death. Thus, convinced
of the wholly human origin of all that is human, a blind man
eager to see who knows that the night has no end, he is still
on the go. The rock is still rolling.

I leave Sisyphus at the foot of the mountain! One always finds one's burden again. But Sisyphus teaches the higher fidelity that negates the gods and raises rocks. He too concludes that all is well. This universe henceforth without a master seems to him neither sterile nor futile. Each atom of that stone, each mineral flake of that night-filled mountain, in itself forms a world. The struggle itself toward the heights is enough to fill a man's heart. One must imagine Sisyphus happy.

EPILOGUE

The preceding merely defines a way of thinking.
But the point is to live.
--Albert Camus